PEAK DISTRICT DIARY

Roger Redfern

Published by Sigma Leisure – an imprint of
Sigma Press, 1 South Oak Lane, Wilmslow, Cheshire SK9 6AR, England.

Whilst every effort has been made to ensure that the information given in this book is correct, neither the publisher nor the author accept any responsibility for any inaccuracy.

British Library Cataloguing in Publication Data
A CIP record for this book is available from the British Library.

ISBN: 1-85058-307-2

Typesetting and Design by: Sigma Press, Wilmslow, Cheshire.

Text photographs: By the author, except where indicated.

Cover photographs: By the author. Left – Ewden Dale from near Bolsterstone, South Yorkshire; right – August afternoon at Unthank Lane Farm, looking across Cordwell Valley, north Derbyshire.

Printed by: Manchester Free Press, Paragon Mill, Jersey Street, Manchester M4 6FP

FOREWORD

by Michael Dower*

It is lovely to have so many of Roger Redfern's short pieces brought together in this volume, with fine photographs of the same creative quality.

Roger Redfern has the eye at once of the painter and of the naturalist. He savours the changing light on the hills, as clouds pass over or the sunlight glints on distant reservoirs; the colours of bracken, peat or snow-shadow; the birds and mountain hares, trees and flowers. He has the historian's nose for ancient tracks and deserted homesteads, cruck barns and the early uses of water power. He writes as if he is *on* the hill, and with a poetic simplicity, as in 'The wet snow draped the deep wood for the first time this winter'.

It is apt that such deep appreciation of the hills should find voice in 'The Guardian', whose writers and photographers have done so much to alert the public to the wonders of the Peak and to animate the cause of public access to the hills and the creation of the Peak National Park. They include Patrick Monkhouse (whose book 'On Foot in the Peak' was first published 60 years ago), Alastair Hetherington, Brian Redhead, and the photographer Denis Thorpe.

Much of the hill country described in this book was not open to the public until very recent years. Manchester folk played a great part in the pre-war campaigns to gain access onto moors from which the public had been excluded by grouse-shooting owners or water companies. These campaigns led to the declaration of the Peak in 1951 as the first National Park, and to the access agreements which opened the moors to the public.

Roger Redfern's joy is to be on the 'empty ground' of the high hills, which he calls the 'real countryside'. He does not enjoy being among the hordes who

* Director General of the Countryside Commission and previously National Park Officer of the Peak District.

rarely stray far from their cars. His walks fall mainly within the Dark Peak of the gritstone; and only a few of these articles celebrate the White Peak, which he calls the 'pallid, anaemic limestone' but which contains some splendid country.

The job of the National Park, however, is to welcome *both* the solitary walkers and the millions who come, year-round, by car to enjoy the valleys as well as the hills of the Dark and the White Peak. As leisure, higher income and car ownership gradually extend through the population, the opportunities for personal refreshment offered by the National Park have never been more needed.

The millions should be welcome. Those who visit the Park will add their voice to the public demand for its protection from the kind of unwise development that Roger Redfern deplores as he faces, for example, the prospect of a major 'improvement' of the road from Sheffield to Manchester through Longdendale. His cry from the heart on this is the tradition of passionate writing from 'The Guardian' about this great southern bastion of the Pennines: 'to think of carrying a broader highway across these delectable heights is crazy, the concoction of the Philistines'.

I thank him for his love of the hills, and his ability to express it for our delight.

Michael Dower

PREFACE

The land-locked hills that are the southern edge of Pennine country have not always enjoyed their present popularity. The high ground was considered dreary, forlorn and storm-tossed, the inhabitants rude and "little removed from savagery". Michael Drayton, Daniel Defoe, Charles Cotton – these and many others thought the Peak District heights toilsome obstacles; and the opinion is understandable.

For the most part, people lived in the countryside, they had no need to seek out other paradises. Those with time and money to travel knew the problems that high, wild country posed. The early "picturesque travellers" which J. B. Firth described in 1905 sought out the beauty of the dales, the moors "wearied and disgusted them". In 1789 Pilkington spoke for the majority when he wrote that "though the moors of Derbyshire are in themselves so unpleasing and disgustful to the imagination, yet they serve by way of contrast to heighten the beauty of the dales and valleys by which they are intersected".

The wholesale industrialisation of the Peak District fringes, both to east and west, concentrated a massive captive population who were just waiting for the chance to break out into the fresh air and sunshine. G. H. B. Ward, Fred Heardman and their contemporaries were the pioneers who led the way. Bert Ward founded the Sheffield Clarion Ramblers in 1900 and so began the great outdoor movement. Now we have great open spaces to explore, and the means to get to them.

Some say we have opened a Pandora's box – the railway brought the first vandals to Peakland, the car brings the multitudes that reduce paths to broad quagmires in popular places, the cult of the mountain bike threatens ancient tracks. Lucky, though, the wanderer who strays into far off country, who still enjoys the quiet hills, distant from car park and gravel path and busy dale. Ghosts of long gone farmers still inhabit curlew moors, far views to distant lowlands are quite unaltered.

My thanks to the family of the late E. Hector Kyme (a lifelong reader of *The Guardian*) for the use of 13 of his photographs.

Roger Redfern

LOCATIONS

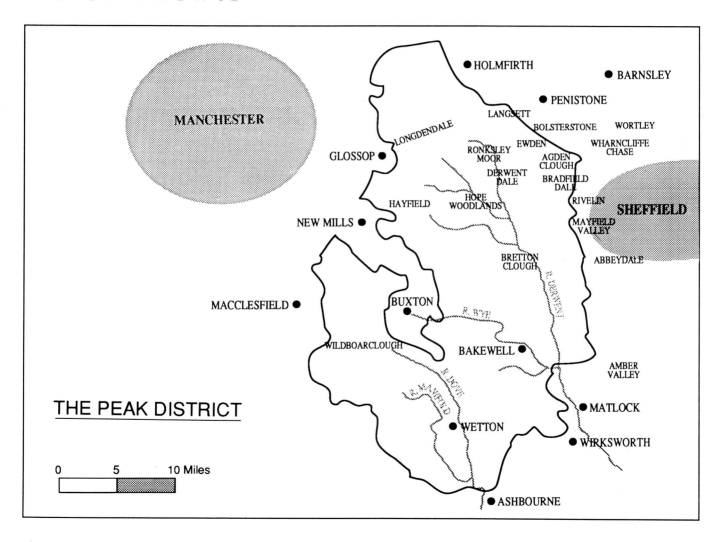

MANCHESTER

HOLMFIRTH

BARNSLEY

PENISTONE

LANGSETT

BOLSTERSTONE   WORTLEY

LONGDENDALE

EWDEN

WHARNCLIFFE
CHASE

GLOSSOP

RONKSLEY
MOOR

AGDEN
CLOUGH

DERWENT
DALE

BRADFIELD
DALE

HAYFIELD

HOPE
WOODLANDS

RIVELIN

MAYFIELD
VALLEY

SHEFFIELD

NEW MILLS

BRETTON
CLOUGH

ABBEYDALE

R. DERWENT

MACCLESFIELD

BUXTON

R. WYE

WILDBOARCLOUGH

BAKEWELL

AMBER
VALLEY

R. MANIFOLD

R. DOVE

MATLOCK

THE PEAK DISTRICT

WETTON

WIRKSWORTH

0   5   10 Miles

ASHBOURNE

CONTENTS

Longdendale, January 1984

At this early end of the year there are days when the low light crosses the hill slopes as at no other season. Pale slants of sunshine pick out the edges of dying nardus and molinia up on Rakes Moss. At 1,650 feet the plateau ends and Laddow Rocks drop vertically towards Crowden Great Brook. The January sun soon turns the corner and this famous gritstone crag returns to chill shadow for another day.

This is the country explored by trespassing climbing pioneers from Manchester at the turn of the century, heralds of the outdoor movement which grew simultaneously on both sides of the Pennines. Here we are certainly on the western, Manchester-facing flank – as evidenced by the five reservoirs filling the floor of Longdendale. By the time of their completion in 1877 they were the largest expanse of artificial water in the world and continue to provide Greater Manchester with twenty four million gallons daily.

Up here, on the crest of Laddow Rocks, you can look down Crowden Great Brook and see the uppermost end of Torside Reservoir but it is the swelling moor that leads the eye north-eastwards to Black Hill's broad back. The pencil line of Holme Moss's television mast never offends me, rising cloudwards not far from Black Hill-top.

On this day, though, we turned back from Laddow's gritty brink, away to the west and over Laddow Moss to the shining water of Chew Reservoir. Here is an unexpected body of water, the highest reservoir in this part of England, constructed between 1907 and 1912. Standing on its bank there is very little to see for you are high on the plateau with only the passing clouds for company. There's little to suggest the presence of the greatest gritstone dale of the southern Pennines just below the reservoir's impounding wall. There it is, though, a huge brown defile with the Chew Brook cascading down below slopes on the scale of a Scottish glen.

Opposite: Chew reservoir, highest reservoir in this part of England

Longdendale, February 1984

Standing on the snow-crested plateau at almost 2,000 feet on a sunny day, I like to watch the antics of the mountain hares. They are difficult to distinguish from the crisp drifts at this season as they bound away under a frosty sky or when blue-grey snow-clouds pile to the north.

It gives me a slight pride to remember at such times that my great uncle, Hardress Dearden, was responsible for introducing the Blue or Mountain Hare to the southern Pennines at the turn of the century. A native of the Highlands, *Lepus timidus scoticus*, has adapted well to the high moors here and rarely a day goes by in this broad country when I don't see several of these gentle, graceful creatures, particularly at this time of year. Their winter coat is highly conspicuous when there's less than usual snow-cover; a greater contrast would be difficult to imagine – silvery hair against dark green of crowberry, burnt brown of ling and chocolate banks of peat. Years ago it was thought that the winter change of coat was like the senile greying of human hair resulting from the activity of chromophages – or colour-eaters. However, a clue that this wasn't the truth came from noting that the tips of a mountain hare's ears remained black, as does the tip of the northern stoat's tail.

By careful experiment it was later established that both northern stoat and mountain hare owe their change of coat colour to a moult triggered, no doubt, by shortening daylight hours in autumn and the lengthening days of spring. What a sighting I had the other day; breasting the craggy rise of Dewhill Naze in a bitter wind I came upon a party of hares sitting round as if out on a picnic. As they casually bounced away across the dark moor-side I silently thanked Hardy for his legacy to the fauna of these Pennine heights.

Opposite: hare tracks above Longdendale (E. Hector Kyme)

Peakland torrent, spring
(E. Hector Kyme)

Longdendale, April 1984

Standing at 1,500 feet beside the Stonefold Spring on the gentle southern slope of Westend Moss I scanned the April sky. What is it that creates the magic on so many spring days? Up here above Crowden Little Brook and Woodhead Reservoir the answer lay obviously in the sky embroidered with silken clouds; the sun now assumes a higher angle, the light intensifies and the world comes alive.

The liquid silver of the spring set me thinking about the demise on these uplands of sphagnum species. Analysis of microscopic spores has shown that they were plentiful on the higher mosses before 1300 but increasing burning to regenerate heather growth and increased atmospheric pollution from south Lancashire since about 1780 has caused their decline. Dr. V. M. Conway proved in 1947 a rainfall pH down to 3.6 in winter – very acid conditions indeed, contaminated by hydrogen chloride, nitrogen dioxide and sulphur dioxide. The latter becomes sulphuric acid in solution and is absorbed by certain cells in sphagnum leaves, causing chlorophyll breakdown and eventual death of the plant.

So sphagnum and other non-flowering plants on these high, broad moors died as the chimneys to the west belched out their poisonous concoctions. While looking on the black side it is interesting to note, too, that the grand little Bog asphodel (Narthecium ossifragum) which brightens so many of the soggy heights of the Highlands is hardly ever seen here. The reason is simple; this little lily doesn't like grazing and the fairly high density sheep population on the Longdendale moors means that it rarely gets a chance to produce its golden flowers between July and September. It used to have the reputation of causing brittle bones in cattle and so earned the specific name "ossifragum" but the lack of calcium carbonate in the soil where it grows best is surely the real cause of the trouble.

Turning now from the Stonefold Spring I went on up the moss, aiming for Black Hill's chocolate summit under that breezy, springtime sky.

*Approaching the Barrow
Stones, Bleaklow Plateau,
summer afternoon*

Longdendale, September 1984

As we breasted the watershed near the Barrow Stones sometime ago I looked northwards across Longdendale to the grey profile of Black Hill; it lay like a snoozing sow, wrapped in heat haze, broad and shapeless and seemed so very far away. I looked again, and looked! There was the dim pencil of the television mast atop Holme Moss – not one mast, though, but two. Were my watering eyes playing tricks in the hot, west wind? It was a relief to hear my companion confirm that he also saw two masts.

Some days later we traversed Dead Edge End and Withens Edge and came to the masts, their tops almost touching the velvet cloud bases. The original mast was built here in 1951 and was the most powerful television transmitter in the world, adding eighteen million viewers to the BBC's audience. Just after completion the 883 rungs of the ladder to the top were climbed by trespassing students; a short time after our recent visit the new 740 feet mast was climbed by that well known son of Bolton, Fred Dibnah, the television steeplejack, by kind permission of the BBC. This new mast radiates mixed polarisation signals to improve reception on radios throughout the north and quite soon the old mast will come down. Holme Moss will assume its three decades-old countenance.

If Fred Dibnah had known where to look from his recent lofty perch he might have picked out the remnants of a sad incident on Twizzle Head Moss, a mile to the south-east. There, on a day of lowering autumn cloud just forty years ago, an American Liberator of 857 Bomber Squadron which had become lost near Holmfirth came to ground. Two local men raced across the soggy moorland in time to see men within the conflagration. It was a desolate pyre for nine crew members. The torn metal lies there still; it is to be hoped that the girders of the first Holme Moss mast are taken away more peremptorily.

Longdendale, December 1984

The wind came whistling on, crashing against the blackened gritstone cliff at our feet; with it came threads of white mist, whizzing by like froth blown off a big river. Gleams of sunlight could be made out far below, where the Greenfield Brook showed through the cloud.

We had come over from Crowden to Chew and saw now, as the wreaths of silver vapour parted, a pike of stones which is the memorial to two local climbers who lost their lives in 1972 while descending the second Sella Tower.

The Climbers' memorial at Dovestones. Bill's O' Jack's Plantation in the distance

Sunbeams and a strong, west wind; mist still raced by as we went along the crest above Dovestone Edge and Dean Rocks. These have long been the Mancunians' beloved crags, soot-encrusted and high and rough textured so that most folk return home after a day here looking like chimney sweeps.

A curtain was raised temporarily and we could see the blackened silhouette of James Platt's Celtic cross, memory of an August day in 1857 when the MP for Oldham was accidentally shot here. Keepers carried him to Ashway Gap House directly below – his brother's country seat – but he died a couple of days later. It must have been prophetic for now Ashway Gap House is no more, recently demolished close beside the new Dove Stone Reservoir.

Then we turned the corner beyond Ashway Rocks and the Ravenstones was directly below us. George Bower of fond memory was one of the pioneers here, discovering soon after 1920 the very severe Wedgewood Crack and named after the instructions he shouted down to his follower – Albert Wood!

This coarse grit crag lacks sunlight at the best of times but at this season it is especially gloomy. Looking down to the muddy waters or out across the chocolate prospect of Middle Edge Moss made me wish heartily for a hard frost and blue skies and new snow. I live in hope.

The memorial to James Platt, looking to Dovestone Edge

9

*Looking up Mickleden Clough
from near Swinden*

Longdendale, January 1985

Which tree grows most successfully to the highest altitude in the South Pennine country? I thought about this the other day as I went up the narrow defile of Crowden Little Brook towards the broad brow of Black Hill and saw the last remnants of former medieval woodland, wind-bent and crack-barked and unhappy hawthorns and rowans. In some major cloughs groups of oak grow surprisingly well and, as in the upper Westend, alders bestow an atmosphere of verdure in sheltered corners.

However, at the limits of tree growth above, say, 1400 feet in windy cloughs only the hawthorn and rowan cling on; and it is the rowan that wins the Hardy Stakes at our latitude. While it forms undergrowth in lowland woodlands and so rarely reaches maturity or is ever seen to bear fruit, it succeeds on the draughty hillside and often attains the stature of a small tree and produces glorious masses of ruby fruit. It was these berries which John Evelyn extolled as making a fine drink and it wasn't without reason that one old-time name for the tree was Hen-drunks for fowls were thought to get intoxicated on the fallen fruit.

The wind-wracked sentinel that now stood high up the clough-side against the winter sky, its silvery bark broken by frost and summer sun, was the highest of all the trees on this part of Black Hill. It grew appropriately close to the tributary of Wiggin Clough for the local name for rowan is "Wiggin", a derivation of witchen or witchwood – in the dim past the tree had magic properties and Pennine folk fastened a branch to the cowshed to keep off the evil eye. There at the wretched, contorted heart of this last rowan on the skyline was the black knot of a twiggy nest, sometime home of a carrion crow, sombre bird of ill-omen whose crackling call echoes at other seasons in the upper cloughs.

One of the holes in "Pots and Pans" on Dick Hill, overlooking the Greenfield Valley

Longdendale, March 1985

You wouldn't expect to find anything of special historic significance on the broad, chocolate brow of Black Hill; 1,908 feet of featureless dome where murky nimbo-stratus so often lurks low and clinging. Imagine the surprise, then, when in 1841 an examination of the summit mound – Soldier's Lump – exposed the large timber framework which had been built there in 1784 to support the 36 inch Great Ramsden theodolite used here as part of the original triangulation of the country.

Jesse Ramsden went from his native Yorkshire to London in 1755. Three years later he became apprenticed to a mathematical instrument maker and seven years later set up in business making astronomical instruments. He soon gained an enviable reputation for the high quality of his products; his celebrated five foot vertical circle speeded up the change from quadrants in observatories.

The actual theodolite used here on Black Hill two centuries ago now stands in the Science Museum and a standard concrete triangulation pillar occupies the same highest point of what has been called "this acid waste". From this plateau-top two important modern routes radiate towards the north-west and north: the former is the ill-defined line of the Pennine Way which in two miles crosses the Greenfield – Holmfirth road near the site of Moors Murders graves, the latter is the more popular Pennine Way Alternative leading by way of Wessenden Head into the reservoir-dotted Wessenden Valley and Marsden, terminus village for walkers of the historic Edale-Marsden (or turn-round point if you are doing the Edale-Marsden Double).

Little of this northern territory is visible from Black Hill's top, though, because it is such a broad dome. Standing up there beside the concrete triangulation pillar you are actually less than a dozen miles from Salterhebble, near Halifax, birthplace of Jesse Ramsden exactly 250 years ago.

Looking north across Stalybridge Road towards Hollingworthhall Moor from Harrop Edge, a walk well-loved by L. S. Lowry

A derelict Pennine farm on Shaw Moor, above Stalybridge

The 1,309 feet summit of Hollingworthhall Moor, looking north to Mossley (left), Buckton Moor and Alphin Pike (right)

Longdendale, April 1985

A dark tongue of hill country pokes south-westward to separate the Tame and Etherow valleys. It hides Stalybridge and Mossley from Mottram and Hollingworth and always looks fascinating from the western hills of Peakland – from, say, Coombes Edge or Peaknaze Moor. Always sombre, it seems, this spur is Hollingworthhall Moor and rises to only 1,309 feet but gives as close a view of the industrial north-west as any hill I know. You look straight down into Dukinfield and Stalybridge and up the serpentine, town-hung dale towards Saddleworth and see the constant comings and goings on Yorkshire – Greater Manchester roads and trains to and from Leeds.

Man has spread far up these heathery, exposed slopes; derelict and blackened hill farms are juxtaposed with small housing estates. Girls ride fat ponies and good lifers tether their goats on neglected pastures surrounded by tumbledown walls. Three-storeyed weavers' cottages climb into the clouds and it's not hard to find what must have been models for some of Laurence Lowry's more rural landscapes, sooty houses on sad moorland. Rain clouds never far away. Yes, this part of the west seems to get more than its fair share of heavy ·cloud, thick stuff that shuts out a lot of sunlight and turns the hill shapes into featureless, half seen outlines. The damp westerlies come this way, of course, rising for the first time on this side of the Pennines so that we usually remember days on Windgate Edge and Hollingworthhall Moor as sunless and grim.

The high voltage power lines strung from towering pylon supports do nothing to enhance the scene, either. They cross from Tintwistle Low Moor to Stalybridge, passing close to the highest part of the hill; the song of the wind in this giant rigging does nothing to soften the character of the place. Occasionally, though, the sky does clear and the sun comes through to light up long distance vistas right across the Cheshire plain, beyond the spread of bricks and mortar and tower blocks to the blue outlines of Welsh hills. Hollingworthhall Moor is, after all, a worthwhile belvedere.

Rock climbing on Agden
Rocher

Agden Clough, June 1985

It always amazes me that one of the finest outcrops in all the Pennines remained so long undiscovered, being one of the last gritstone edges to be developed. It is little more than thirty years ago that Eric Byne, our High Peak King of fond memory, came first to Agden Rocher and saw its potential for further extensive exploration.

Since that time this lovely crag has been criss-crossed and girdled, gardened and dusted down so that there can be little left to find. That doesn't matter, though, because the Rocher lies in such a delectable position – high above Agden and draped about with its own oak wood where cuckoos are calling now.

The Rocher is the result of a great landslip in the long ago, revealing a grand exposure of Huddersfield White Rock rearing vertically to a hundred feet and offering better, square-cut holds than most types of gritstone. The other day, while traversing across the face, I almost trod on a fox as he peered out of his lair and padded off nonchalantly through the clinging oaks. A couple of minutes later he was trotting across the sward far below, twisting this way and that between grazing ewes and lambs, everyone unconcernedly going about their own business.

If, though, modern man overlooked this outcrop his predecessors didn't and by going to the eastern end of the wood you will find Bowsen Barn, all that remains of an ancient farm. It stands upon a tree-girdled knoll commanding Agden Clough and its reservoir. Tumbled stones and fragments of oak beams represent the house but the medieval cruck barn stands as solid as ever. As evidence of occupation at an even earlier time are the round and horseshoe scrapers and trimmed flakes found in a field below the Rocher on a day in 1888. They are Neolithic or, possibly, early Bronze Age and were fashioned from what may well be horse bone by men who listened, no doubt, to the ancestors of the cuckoos which are now calling in these very oaks.

The infant Don (E. Hector Kyme)

Longdendale, December 1985

Here we are at the shortest day of the year, when we have scarcely time to get up onto the highest ground and look around before the western sky is seamed with orange or pink. It was just such a time of day that I came last week to the line of mounds on Upper Dead Edge. All about was the sullen heather moor, a dark and dirty brown under blankets of blue-grey cloud roll.

The water oozing between each tussock soon trickles off to the north-east and forms the infant Don, major river of South Yorkshire. I looked down its shallow, early valley and saw a break in the cloudy gloom; quite soon the cloud was parting to reveal a pale, cold sky over Penistone way. It was one of those wondrous winter afternoons, a dark day metamorphosing to bright evening.

A mile and a half away to the north I could now see the mound of Cook's Study Hill, site of the long gone Cook's Study, a folly of the Stanhope estate used as a shooting lodge. Before the end it was burnt out and haunted, now a few stones on the tiny hillock are all that remain.

A mile across the moor the other way the gaunt finger of ruinous tower that is a former ventilation shaft of the first Woodhead railway tunnel poked against the last clouds. You could imagine those cloud remnants as blowing smoke from some ghost train passing deep under the ground in what was, when built in 1845, the longest tunnel in the world.

Golden shafts slanted out across the broad landscape of West and South Yorkshire, the dingy haze was dissipated to leave a clear prospect of the promised land. Looking west down Longdendale the cloud belt was broken long enough to let red slashes of sundown through, reflected a thousand times on the rippling surfaces of that dale's reservoir chain.

Looking back towards Crowden Great Brook from upper Wildboar Clough

Longdendale, January 1986

Just before the first proper snow of the winter we were traversing on a cold and sunny day below Robinson's Moss, where the silvery water comes splashing down from 1,700 feet and through the mini-gorge of Lad's Leap. We were quite out of the north-easterly wind here and stood awhile to absorb the tepid sunshine rays. Across the steep-sided ravine the blood-red bracken punctuated a rocky slope where a few ewes were also taking the sun. My eye caught a sudden brilliance near the sheep and, looking closer, I could see a white form on the grass; a gull had landed – or had it?

Funny sort of time and place for gulls, despite the ribbon of reservoirs along the valley-floor. Then I saw another brilliant blob nearer the plateau-crest. We watched for any slight motion but saw none. Across the silver cascade and below the blood-red bracken bank and up on all fours I came to a perfect hide behind a gritty boulder and only then saw the nearest mountain hare. It sat twenty feet above me, ears flat along its back and pale blue eyes watching my silly, futile antics; only when I attempted to draw even closer did it stand on its back legs and bounce casually up the slope, confident that it could out-pace most living things on any uphill grade.

Lepus timidus scoticus may change its coat as the day length shortens but it's so good at travelling these adopted uplands that its conspicuousness doesn't give it sleepless nights. Then when the snow comes properly it's really laughing.

Only the other day we came again to that slope below Robinson's Moss, kicking steps in the firm snow slope. There might have been a dozen mountain hares watching our laboured progress. but we never saw them. What I did notice, though, was the gorgeous play of light on the frozen surface of Valehouse Reservoir eight hundred feet below, and drifts of powder snow blown across the ice by the curling wind.

The source of the
Derbyshire Derwent, above
Swain's Greave, Bleaklow

Longdendale, February 1986

On a doubtful morning of inky clouds racing across the heights, driven by an angry west wind, we went up beside the infant Derwent over remnants of snow-ice. Sheets of the blue stuff made progress tricky, mocked as we went by an occasional grouse skimming the blackened heather mounds.

At last we came down by Far Black Clough where the stream was racing to join the Etherow near the site of lonely, long-gone Woodhead station. A gusty wind was screaming up Longdendale and we found no shelter at the tunnel portals; the prospect of the long traverse of soggy Longside Moss and Dearden Moss to Dunford Bridge was unattractive. There was a better alternative and so we strode off into the heart of the hills, through the concrete bore of the last Woodhead Tunnel.

Constructed parallel to the twin bores of the original tunnels – they were the longest in the world when opened to traffic in 1845 and 1852 – the new tunnel came into use in 1954 to carry electric – hauled traffic. I well remember its remarkable interior seen from the window of the train for, unlike most tunnels, its walls were bright and clean and lit by electric lights. As we walked through the other day the steel hooks for those remembered lights were still in place. We were warm and dry as we went along, cocooned by mother earth from the stormy day outside. Nearly halfway along we saw ghostly light to the right, and echoing waters; we looked far up the dank ventilation shaft where drainage from the Etherow head-waters was cascading in silver ribbons.

In an hour and ten minutes we were out of this third longest British railway tunnel, into the gusting wind again and heading over the Thurlstone Moors for Flouch cross-roads. In failing light we aimed up ancient Cut Gate, towards Derwent Dale. Heavy squalls of horizontal hail now made progress slow as we floundered through soft drifts on the 1,725 feet watershed and torches were needed on the steep descent to Slippery Stones and the sheltering arms of Ronksley Plantation – two havens on a stormy day, both man-made.

In Wildboar Clough,
summer

26

Longdendale, June 1986

The cuckoo was reluctant to call in the high cloughs this spring. Sheets of shower-rain drifted across the moor-tops, rainbows flashed from farm to farm when the sun saw fit to come out from behind the copious cloud layers and we continued to plough a soggy furrow through the mosses of our beloved plateau country.

On a particularly inauspicious grey morning we came over by Birchen Bank Moss to the scattered trees in Stable Clough, bright green in new-burst foliage despite the weather. Taking shelter by a pile of gritstone boulders as another squall came hissing out of the west we could gaze across the head of Woodhead Reservoir to where little Pikenaze Hill must have been. Low cloud and diagonal shafts of rain hid the hill completely.

Quite suddenly, though, the rain stopped, the clouds parted and the sun sent gorgeous light flooding right across the far side of the dale. Pikenaze glistened in the brilliance and a great rainbow arch cut the black sky towards Holme Moss. The new birch and rowan leaves shone over our heads and, as if to order, a cuckoo began his call lower down our own clough. We relaxed in the warmth and marvelled at the landscape transformation before traversing west among the fallen boulders of Dovestone Rocks and Deer Knowl. The light remained good and cuckoos continued their calling as we came round the great tumbled mass of rock called Rollick Stones at the mouth of Wildboar Clough where the stream comes cascading through perhaps the finest rocky defile in all Peakland, draining this portion of northern Bleaklow.

At this season the plateaux surfaces take on their loveliest countenance, assuming a patchwork effect of burgeoning greens and yellows as bilberry and crowberry send out their latest foliage. Bracken breaks out in luscious banks on some clough-sides. Our grey daybreak had metamorphosed to a fabulous early summer midday in response, it seemed, to the cuckoo's clarion call.

The lower entrance to
Wildboar Clough, Bleaklow.

Evening on Dovestone Reservoir, with Dick Hill beyond

*The shooting cabin on
Broomhead Moor,
overlooking Side Head Beck*

Ewden, October 1986

In the middle of last month I came across Broomhead Moor; the strong sunshine lit up the ling to perfection. It was a regal carpet. The broad, purple slope dazzled the eyes and heightened the contrast with its margin of bracken where the moor falls suddenly towards the upper dale. I was gathering cowberries (or red whortleberry) where they grow profusely at the edge of the moor, close to the Bronze Age stone circle only re-discovered a few years ago after a moor fire had destroyed the heather and bracken.

As I went along, treading the purple carpet, I overtook a bee-keeper making his way to hives beside a wall. Like many northern apiarists, he brings his colonies up here each early August for a six weeks' holiday, during which time they gorge themselves on the sweet nectar of a million ling blooms. "They don't need any sugar-feeding, in the winter when they've been up here," he reminded me as he stuck his head under a veiled hat and lit the cardboard in his smoke gun.

"You don't want to bother with cowberry jelly," he advised, "all that sugar's bad for you. Get some honey down yer instead!" Soon I was out of sight and picking the last of what has been an indifferent season for moor-fruits. The bilberries were quite plentiful but these cowberries are smaller than usual and so take a lot more time to pick. It was a typically golden autumn afternoon with sailing cumulus, droning flies and a few wandering honey bees; the occasional pop of distant shotguns meant that a party was taking grouse higher up the purple moor.

When I went back the bee-keeper had gone home but his insects were busy at work, making good use of each golden hour of their holiday.

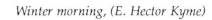

Amber Valley, December 1986

There's little surprise that early winter landscapes are among my favourites when I remember a recent Saturday morning spent in the Amber Valley. A bright sun shone and a cold wind blew as I crossed the pastures below Brackenfield. Friesians were grazing the park-like sward near Ogston Hall and tall beeches stood like towers of burnt sienna. A curl of blue smoke lifted from a thicket where a farming family were cleaning up fallen branches and sawing logs. They thanked me for mentioning that "Mallard" was due to pass in half an hour – my reason for crossing those fields towards South Wingfield, where the main line runs in delightful, undiscovered country between gently swelling hills.

Coming from Marylebone this train was carrying £55-a-head passengers to York via Banbury and Derby. It would be the longest steam-hauled journey in Britain for eighteen years. The world record breaking locomotive would be uncoupled at York and returned to the Railway Museum for the winter while the excursion went back to London behind a mere diesel.

The cold wind blew, the cloud rolls came out of the west to hide the sun. It would be a matter of luck if the train passed in brilliance or in shade. Then, at 1.15 p.m., and shaking with cold and inactivity I saw white rolls of cloud rising above the dark skeleton forms of trees in the south. Soon the unmistakable, proud-chested front of an A4 hurtled onto the embankment, a bright blue wedge shining in the full sun and hissing gently at 60 mph. Click, click, click went my shutter and the long train had passed, leaving spirals of smoke and steam to drift over the fields to Higham.

Suddenly it came to me. I was standing in those very fields that once I used to look out upon from the carriage window on my way home from college, at just this time on Saturdays. Smoke and steam drifted by those windows as an unremarkable matter of course; it was unimaginable then that one day – thirty four years on – I would be standing down there to watch what has become such a rare spectacle.

Longdendale, January 1987

The distant rumble of trains on the electrified Woodhead line used to be a pleasant feature of descents from the high plateaux, on the way down Torside Clough or Crowden Great Brook or the dozens of other ways of reaching the dale from Bleaklow and Black Hill. Groping down sodden heather tussocks in the last light of a winter's afternoon you could stand for a moment to watch the distant line of lights go by – an express bound for Sheffield Victoria, may be – before continuing valley-wards into deepening gloom made that much worse by those passing lights. All that came to an end more than fifteen years ago but hopes had recently been raised that BR might re-open the Woodhead line.

They are now dashed with the latest announcement that the route is never likely to carry traffic again. An extra nail has been driven into the coffin with North West Water's scheme to re-inforce and deepen some of the reservoirs that fill Longdendale's floor. A century ago – when completed – they formed the largest expanse of reservoirs in the world, the continuing monument to J. F. Bateman's skill and tenacity as an engineer who worked here for four decades. Despite their sound construction the proposed re-inforcement work is designed to ensure that they withstand the sort of flash flood which happens only "once in ten thousand years".

Coming down off Westend Moss the other day we traversed Hey Edge and so came in sight of the lowering sun far out over the western plain; Bateman's string of lakes glinted pink and gold as the frost sank to the dale-bottom and silken vapours condensed to clinging mist. There was a far calling of gulls on Torside and an arrow flight of mallard went across the coloured sky – but no welcome rumble on the Woodhead rails, no distant line of lights bound for Sheffield Victoria.

*Early spring at Wiremill
Dam, Mayfield Valley,
looking to the hilltop site of
Whiteley Wood Hall*

Mayfield Valley, February 1987

Of the roughly 2 million hectares supporting one million horses in this country a large proportion are semi-derelict, dock-dotted pastures, often punctuated with painted oil drums and tumbled shacks. Coming down this steep little valley below the hanging woods of Porter Clough the other day I looked at the dumpy pastures touched with gold where the low sun caught the last dried grass flowers. Beyond that burnished dome stood the grey pony which has so long haunted this corner of the dale, with him half a dozen Friesian yearling heifers arranged themselves, grouped as only Arnesby Brown would place them on their sunlit knob.

This was old horse pasture par excellence. Far down the valley reared pale Sheffield towers, far enough away to look romantic from this silent corner where pony and his elegant pals were dreaming. Though affluent Victorian and Edwardian merchants and industrialists built their substantial dwellings ever higher up these slopes Mayfield has never really lost its rural countenance. Only a handful of stone farms and cottages impinge here, remnants of a quieter time when the city's only real industry saw men at water-powered grinding hulls like the preserved Shepherd Wheel lower down this valley.

It's not always so gentle here, of course. Twenty five years ago tomorrow, for instance, the Great Sheffield Gale screamed off the western heights and down these declivities at almost one hundred miles an hour to play havoc with chimneys, roofs, whole houses.

On this recent day, though, all was peace as we wandered down to Carr Bridge and beyond. I cast an eye up to White House Farm where, long ago, Stanley Royle lived in a caravan in the yard as an adopted son of the city, never fully recognised as a major artist in his lifetime.

Bowsen Barn, Agden
Rocher

Agden Rocher, above
Bradfield Dale

Agden Clough, April 1987

Great cauliflowers of cloud reared in the sky as we went up by Grindle Barn to the russet moor. The ash trees below the barn have that silver sheen about their twigs now, precursor of green buds and cuckoo call. The trio of gritstone buildings were put here on their tiny shelf exactly three hundred and forty years ago, perched on this fearsome pasture grade almost overhanging, it seems, the cascade in Grindle Clough.

It's many long years since hay was stored here by the resident of High House, or calves fastened up for the winter. There are still, though, the remains of manure in Grindle Barn and a horse rake and mowing machine under the adjacent wind-bent sycamore. Quiet remnants of quieter times.

Having crossed the watershed near White Tor we tramped the heather moor down to the meanders and shale banks of Strines Dike and so came through the giant beech trees to Mortimer Road in Bradfield Dale. In the early afternoon we climbed above Agden Reservoir to the cruck barn of Bowsen, sleeping still below its girdling trees at the southern end of Agden Rocher.

The sun continued to shine and, here among the twisted little oaks, the chill spring breeze had died. We climbed up the square-cut holds of Huddersfield White rock which form Agden Rocher and sat on the crest where all the wide world seemed visible. There were larks in the sky over West Nab but no human was abroad on this magic, silent day. I lay back on the tussock grass, legs hanging over the Rocher's rim. High overhead as I gazed the cauliflower clouds were piled like fairy castles in the blue; was it possible that I heard the Shearing piano? Maybe only skylarks far away.

Langsett, June 1987

There's a part of the upper Porter Valley which has more landscape affinity with the eastern Highlands than the south Pennines. As you come down from the high western country of Cloudberry Moor into the upper clough the first wiggin and birch trees decorate the stream-side, causing the young bracken shoots to grow taller in their lee than out on the moor.

We bounced down to Scarratt's Stone and along to the sheep-fold, that spot blessed by generations of hill wanderers and sheep men alike for its windbreak effect. Just downstream is the site of Hordron Cabin which has saved more than one life in the drifting snows of a winter night but recently destroyed by sick-minded vandals in the name of animal rights.

Up the green hill pasture again, to Upper Hordron – outlying barn and simple dwelling but long since abandoned. Hordron Cabin's demise has seen Upper Hordron's resurrection, recently re-roofed to shelter beaters and shots in the coming season. It is beyond Hordron, though, that the Porter takes on its Highland look for a mile or so before it flows into Langsett Reservoir; and the thing which makes it so is the grouping of old trees, particularly Scots pines which emulate a remnant of the Caledonian Forest near, say, Derry Lodge. Up the sunny slope beyond were the waving tops of the sycamores encircling abandoned Swinden twin farms, great green towers. A secret path twists up through the dark ankles of the conifers to come out by the ruins and on across a broad, re-seeded pasture. We traversed a silver rivulet here, edged with a row of bird cherries, their shiny leaves turning in the stiff breeze, their impossibly beautiful spikes of white flowers bending, too, against the blue sky. It seemed such a waste, no-one to gaze on their transient glory up in the lonely country. Then a cuckoo called from the ruins of Far Swinden Farm – we weren't alone.

Old cart shed, Swinden
Farm

At the Barrow Stones,
looking northeast to the
South Yorkshire lowlands.

Ronksley Moor, August 1987

Drifting rain sheets hid the far moor-top as we went up beside the Westend River, its peaty water galloping down towards the dripping conifers of the first plantation. It seemed no time at all since we last came this way, under a bright, blue sky with the sun burning our backs. The river then was a trickle, whispering its way over those gritstone steps which make this dale such an attractive place. By the time we'd reached the stand of ancient alders in Dry Clough the clouds were breaking and a gliding curlew was herald to the first sunbeam on the distant Grinah Stones.

In the hour it takes to go up from the Westend's mouth at Howden-side to the great sculptured Barrow Stones the day had evolved from dismal grey to shining blue. The Barrow Stones are a surprisingly good viewpoint over the South Yorkshire lowlands and now we could see the man-made towers of cumulus at Ferrybridge, twenty eight miles away, and Drax, thirty eight miles away, to the north-east. In the clearest conditions York Minster's towers are visible forty-five miles across the flatlands and some say Lincoln's triple towers can be picked out, the best part of sixty miles distant but I can't verify this.

Remote as the Barrow Stones are we could hear the distant drone of traffic on the Woodhead road, where it crosses the high watershed at 1,500 feet near the place called Fiddler's Green. I remembered the story of Matthew Hinchcliffe (Mat o' Nacks), tenant of the Plough and Harrow at that lonely high point of the pass, who intercepted a navvy at the time of the first Woodhead Tunnel's construction· in the act of stealing a goose. The landlord shot the thief in the legs and followed the trail of blood towards the tunnel mouth but the navvy was never seen again.

Then the drone of traffic was drowned by the nearer drone of hover flies circling in the afternoon heat above us as we lay and gazed afar.

Looking down Dimpus Clough towards the upper Sett Valley from the summit of South Head (1,622 ft). Cown Edge is on the left horizon.

Hayfield, October 1987

Over many years' observation it has been established that the days around October 25th coincide with the pinnacle of autumn colour in this country. Despite seasonal and regional variation this time is, on average, the best for the outward manifestation of chemical change within deciduous foliage throughout the land.

The silver birches of Glen Affric take some beating when the sun comes from behind the October clouds with shafts of pure light reflected from the mirror surfaces of Lochs Affric and Beinn a Mheadhoin in the high country beyond the Great Glen. Nearer home, though, the moorland shines under blue skies, great yellow swathes of grass tilt to little cloughs where the bronzed bracken almost hides tiny, bouldery cascades and the highest wiggins survive just below the blasted moor-top. Mention of the wiggin reminds me that a recent correspondent asked for a translation of this ancient name; for wiggin read rowan, usually highest sited of all trees in this region.

A year ago we came down off Chunal Moor towards Hollinworth Head and saw Chunal Plantation painted vivid red. At first glance it seemed we had come on the very best day to see the flaming foliage on these moor-side rowans but on closer inspection it was clear that not a single leaf remained, what we saw were a million vermilion berries catching the chilly October sunlight. I have never seen a better display of Peakland wiggins, and the spectacle underlined the fact that the ash-like leaves present autumn glory only briefly, soon to be ripped off the tree in the first strong wind. Just beyond Hollinworth Head lies the gritstone remnant of the Abbot's Chair in the lane-side verge, really a boundary stone and way marker on this Monk's Road which climbs over the flank of Coombes Edge before dropping westwards to Charlesworth with broad and thrilling views over Greater Manchester where distant smoke curls here and there alluringly.

*The ruins of North
America farm, near
Langsett*

Langsett, December 1987

The shortest days are here again and have their compensations. When the conditions are right we can hardly fail to admire the sunset banners of dying day long before getting down from high places. It's good, too, when we walk on through the failing light of dusk and on into the monochrome world of night with a moon rising higher as we go lower into the apparent blackness of the dale.

On the evening of the recent full moon we returned from a day on the heathery tops and came into such an inky glade at Swinden. Shafts of silver sliced the grassy path as we went, forming a bright trellis where moonshine was broken by a thousand spruce trunks. This is the blanket plantation country which has overwhelmed the pretty, walled pastures of the long abandoned farms above Brook House Bridge where the Little Don meanders down to Langsett village. There wasn't a breath of wind as we went along the magic glade, only a branch rustling as a tawny owl winged low past us from its pinnacle perch against the moon. Far off up the clough a fox barked under the stars as we went on and, leaving the last trees, headed again for the open moors and the far road-head beyond Slippery Stones.

The moonlight was reflected from Langsett Reservoir's glassy surface a mile to the east, beyond the abandoned hill pastures of tumbled North America Farm. Formerly called Maukroyd its tenant was cleared away long ago, maybe relieved that his burden of scratching a living from this unforgiving, short-season territory was lifted. Most of it is now heathery and grazed by a few wiry hill ewes, between tumbled gritstone walls.

An hour later we had crossed the 1,750 feet watershed and came down the steep way to the dark, enfolding arms of the conifers about Slippery Stones. Brilliance was again visible through the black prison bars of spruce – liquid silver on Howden Reservoir's surface towards the King's Tree.

Langsett, February 1988

Opposite: Gritstone tor on Howden Edge, (E. Hector Kyme)

The long dip slope which rolls away eastwards from the tor-dotted crest of Derwent Edge and Howden Edge is misleadingly uniform; especially so in the poor, grey light of a cloudy winter's day. The shallow, boggy trenches which descend towards Bradfield Dale and the Ewden Valley are hard to recognise without far-away reference points – like the tower of Boot's Folly and Bolsterstone parish church.

More than seventy years ago a navvy who had been employed on the building of Howden Reservoir in Derwent Dale found himself without work and so decided to cross this high ground to seek work on dams being built in the Little Don Valley. Local residents advised against the journey; it was a winter afternoon with the weather fast deteriorating. He didn't heed the warning and set off eastwards on the Cut Gate track but never reached Langsett. His disappearance remained a mystery until late the following summer when a shooting party discovered his rotten corpse in a heather-shrouded grough where he must have sought shelter in the blizzard that overtook him.

It's on the broad, plain-like moorlands that most danger lurks in winter for the unprepared, not on the craggy edges. Confused stumblings in the quagmire head-waters of the Ewden Beck can soon sap energy from wanderers without a map or the means to locate their position.

But conditions couldn't have been much better for us the other day as we traversed from Lord Edward Howard's Spring below Crow Stones Edge and came over the broad top of Margery Hill, highest place in South Yorkshire. There were broken white clouds over the far lowlands where Ferrybridge, Eggborough and Drax were sending their own towering cumulus heavenwards, at our feet the peat shone with fragile ice sheets, sparkling in the sunshine. A flock of white pigeons came racing by, turning as one bird this way and that, far from their loft in, maybe, Loxley or Wharncliffe Side.

Hope Woodlands, March 1988

Opposite: Spring snow near the top of Grindsbrook, with Grindslow Knoll behind.(E. Hector Kyme)

Deep blue clouds came in on the north wind as we crossed the southern edge of the Kinder Scout plateau from Edale Head Rocks towards the top of Grindsbrook Clough where the Pennine Way clambers up onto the peaty table-top en route for Bleaklow and the Scottish border. The sun came out just as we crossed the babbling infant brook, where it curls down runnels smoothed through the generations before that quick descent to the Vale of Edale. A shining wall of snow-ice reared to one side, firm enough to kick steps in a pleasant traverse above the deepening gorge.

Behind our winter playground on the brink of the plateau is the level site of what was the Peak District's highest shooting cabin – Four Jacks it was called and stood at 1,965 feet. Gamekeeper Mike Tym of Edale built the original cabin for the Campions of Grindslow House. A staunch Methodist Mike had his occasional lapses into strong drink but saw the error of his ways and took the opportunity of preaching on the evils of alcohol to the labourers helping him to construct this elevated cabin. Thereafter it was known as Micah's

Church. Later rebuilding with the luxury of two compartments – for guns and beaters respectively – by four men with the Christian name Jack meant that it became Four Jacks cabin.

I can remember this low-built hut beside the gravel meanders of the brook some way up from the ravine, just before vandals smashed it up and estate staff finally removed all traces of it; the sportsman's loss was also the ramblers' for the cabin had always offered shelter in bad weather, now there's none here.

As we went on, the grey hump of a mountain hare showed where it crouched on a gravel bed, hoping to be inconspicuous, but its nerve soon broke and we watched it lope off towards the top of Blackden Rind. Then we came to the brink of Blackden Edge and looked down to the scattered farms and landslip country of the Woodlands as snow started to come out of darker clouds.

Wharncliffe Lodge

Wharncliffe Chase, April 1988

We crossed the high, rolling parkland above the broken gritstone edge of Wharncliffe Crags where cumulus galleons sailed in the early April blue. Up here on the 1,000 feet contour this is hard country with magnificent prospects into the deep and wooded declivities of the Don Valley on one side and far across the eastern lowlands on the other. In good conditions York Minster and Lincoln Cathedral are visible over forty miles away.

Whancliffe Lodge stands splendidly on its gritstone crag with a sheer prospect down the woods to the Don; built by Sir Thomas Wortley in 1510 it served as a hunting lodge and later as a residence for the Wortleys while their great house at Wortley was altered in 1800. I searched the crag-tops for several years to locate the celebrated Inscription Rock of 1510 commemorating Sir Thomas, only to find it eventually protected by railings inside the Lodge. The Chase rears behind the old house with scattered plantings of sycamore and beech which have survived surprisingly well considering the bleak exposure. Here roamed North American bison in the last century, a romantic touch in this prairie-like setting, highest of all parklands. The pregnant Countess Wharncliffe went over one day from Wortley to the Lodge by carriage and her small dogs chased a bison. Soon the herd turned the tables and charged the carriage, putting the horses to flight. The excitement resulted in a miscarriage for the Countess so the herd was later shot. Until recently the mounted head of the last Wharncliffe bison hung at the Lodge but was stolen on a snowy day and has not been recovered. Archibald Ralph, 3rd Earl Wharncliffe (1892-1953), a life-long Guardian reader, would not have been amused.

*Looking north-east to
Hollin Brown Knoll and
Greenfield Reservoir from
Bill's O' Jack's plantation
below the A625.*

Longdendale, May, 1988

Once more the cuckoo's call sounds across the still-brown bracken banks above the head-waters of Etherow, Don and Little Don here on England's central watershed. It is spring and on some days, in the lee of rocks where the eastern wind can't bluster, there's even a feel of early summer. We looked down from Bleaklow's northern rim into the dale where pale sheep were grazing on Pikenaze Hill and the Woodhead road curved beside the glinting reservoir. Poised on the top of the crags at Deer Knowl we looked almost vertically down upon the new-burst foliage of the uppermost rowans which grow scattered across the boulder field of fallen blocks brought down by countless frosts from our cliff face.

On such a day as this it puts fresh heart into one to look across the greatest of all south Pennine dales to the multi-coloured slopes that rear to Chew and Black Hill and Holme Moss; a broad landscape where the curlew is king under floating islands of cloud and the dunlin nestles low on its lone nest in the cotton grass. It was just possible to make out the line of the path which climbs from Crowden, in the dale-bottom, by Loftend Quarry and up by Westend Moss and White Low to the far tops of Black Hill. This is one of the alternatives of the Pennine Way and increasing wear will do no favours for this wide moor-side. Better, I think, to keep the crowds to the broad highway of beaten track which goes up by Laddow Rocks and Crowden Great Brook to Black Hill than cause wider havoc on this fragile, mossy, often oozing terrain of Westend and White Low.

With the Heart of England Way now being prepared, linking Land's End with Scotland, this part of the Pennine Way may well receive increased usage – and damage. It's a pity we can't fly over our beloved hill shapes; curlew and dunlin don't leave murky trails across these dusky heights.

The pinnacle on Dovestone Edge

Wetton, June 1988

The clear, bright light of early June brings out the new colours of the hanging deciduous woods of Dovedale and on a recent morning we climbed up by the ancient lime kiln on the fringe of Hurt's Wood. The bluebell haze sent heavenly aroma around the gigantic beech boles that cling at crazy angles to the craggy side of Hall Dale.

We came out onto the sheep-shorn crests of the limestone ridge where meadow saxifrage blooms were nodding their white heads in the west wind; on damper spots some way down the cliff we soon found colonies of Early Purple Orchis and great, yellow drifts of cowslips shining in the sunshine.

At Air Cottage we peered down five hundred feet onto the multi-coloured tree-tops overhanging the hidden Dove where it bubbles past Reynard's Cave and the sharp limestone needles of Tissington Spires. A flock of ducks did the conga across the stack-yard, a pet lamb nuzzled us for its milk bottle, a lark trod the air far overhead; otherwise the world seemed empty.

As we went on to the south by Bunster Hill the ridge narrowed to a grassy arete, culminating in the spur-end called Dovedale Castle. Here you look across the actual mouth of Dovedale to the sharp pyramid of Thorpe Cloud (942 feet); it is the place that the Dove leaves its deep dale for gentler, pastoral countryside, the very southern limit of the Pennines. There are few airier places in this part of England, great space on three sides and a broad vista over green ridges away to the Midlands. Then we looked vertically down and saw the road-head car park jammed with vehicles and crowds strolling a few hundred yards to the stepping-stones. What a relief that the hordes rarely stray far from their cars; we're still able to easily loose them all after a short climb into the real countryside.

*Anglers beside the River
Dove (E. Hector Kyme)*

Looking down Ewden Dale from Moorside Cottage at the edge of Broomhead Moor. Broomhead Reservoir fills the dale-floor and Bolsterstone village stands on the far hilltop (centre).

The ancient cruck barn at Dwarriden – "the dwarf's dean" or "hollow"

Ewden, July 1988

The rhododendron blooms have now faded at Broomhead, last survivors of the once-grand grounds of that great moor-edge home of the Rimmington Wilsons. Behind them is the sweep of what was probably the finest of all grouse moors, below is the deep trough of Ewden Dale, banked with dark woods and tilting pastures and pretty farms beside secret, twisting lanes.

Myrtle Downing recently recounted to me how she and her brother and sisters had spent happy days at Aunty Kitty's remote Rochner Head Farm in the adjacent Bradfield Dale and how her father-in-law started work at the age of seven in the gardens of Broomhead Hall. This first job was digging daises out of the lawns, later graduating to general duties in the greenhouses filled with peaches, nectarines, grapes, figs and tomatoes.

Looking across Ewden Dale from, say, Waldershaigh, Broomhead Park still presents a brave countenance, tree-dotted pasture sweeping down towards the dark waters of Broomhead Reservoir. But there is no big house now; after lying derelict for years Broomhead was flattened and the family stay in an adjacent estate cottage during their periodic visits to this northern outpost nine hundred feet above the sea.

The summer drought of 1933 shrank the waters of the reservoir sufficiently to reveal the arch of the old Broomhead Mill Bridge and remains of the zinc sulphide and lead workings below it which were in use between 1647 and 1815. Overlooking the south side of the reservoir was Dwarriden Farm, home of the Ronksleys for two and a half centuries until 1935. Like so many dam-side dwellings this lovely old place has been totally razed in the so called interest of clean drinking water, only its cruck barn stands, lonely where hens once scratched and the calls of farm children echoed round a stackyard now taken over entirely by nettles and briars. Further on is ancient Jack Lane and Bank Side, embowered at present with pink waves of dog roses and heavily scented with apricot blooms of the honeysuckle which has clambered here these past thousand years.

Looking south-west from the edge of Wharncliffe Chase across the Don Valley to Onesmoor. Wharncliffe Lodge is on the left.

Wortley, July 1988

We came up from the east, through woodlands and along leafy lanes, mounting steadily through Wortley Park to the ridge-top village at 750 feet above the sea. It was a day of dark-sided clouds and brilliant sunshine and now we could look out over the huge, dappled valley of the Don. Beyond that hollow of multi-coloured fields and the dark sprawl of Stocksbridge rise the high moors of the south Pennines, wide sweeps of brown with blue shadows under this racing sky.

The ridge at Wortley is a sort of boundary separating the whale back country and green woods that slope beyond Wentworth to the coalfield from the heaving territory of delectable hills which are ranged across the western horizon. The village catches every wind that blows but on a soft day in the middle of the year, as now, its refreshing breezes are welcome. Few flies reside at Wortley. Embowered in its leafy park is the grand Hall, home of the Wharncliffes for four centuries until 1950, since when it has been a rest home. Standing by the herbaceous borders it was hard to im-agine the winter blast that often sweeps the ridge-top a few hundred yards to the west.

Looking again to the Don Valley the orange gash of a great cutting recently inflicted on the end of Wharncliffe Chase was conspicuous. It carries the new Stocksbridge by-pass and its coming inflicted dust and disturbance near Earl Wharncliffe's back door in his last days. Now the road is open it has brought serious traffic congestion to Grenoside and other settlements north of Sheffield. The sandwich layers of that gaudy cutting above the Don will, in time, mellow as water streaks it and willowherb and stonecrop take root; the headlong race of traffic bound ever faster towards narrow roads will continue, moving the queues but not really curing them.

Langsett, September 1988

A recent correspondent and Guardian reader for sixty years would, I'm sure, have enjoyed our day on the purple moor-carpets of Midhope and Langsett. We came over from the Derwent by Cut Gate and admired the broad cornlands that seem to clothe most of South Yorkshire at this time of year, golden sheets broken only by hill-top woods and capped by the far line of man-made cumulus at Ferrybridge, Eggborough and Drax.

From the Flouch, where George Heward was the first landlord before Victoria came to the throne, we mounted Bord Hill beside the ever-busy Woodhead highway before turning across Loftshaw and Cloudberry Moor, wading knee-deep through the purple heather pile. At Laund Clough, where the brook cascades innocently for a long way down tilting gritstone beds, we parted the bracken to look once again at Scarratt's Stone. It brought back memories of shooting parties here a century ago led by the Sheffield cutler George Howson who owned the shooting rights at that time. His friend Scarratt came up from London for the sport each autumn between 1887 and 1897 and would rest just here on the way to the butts so Howson had this stone inscribed to honour the old chap in 1894.

Turning up towards the empty top of Harden Moss we came to the Hoar Stones and gazed out from this place where so many streams have their gentle birth in the peaty ooze. The occasional cotton grass bloom was still nodding and a mountain hare bounced off over the purple horizon. Soon we came up to the lonely Horse Stone, only sentinel on this 1,700 feet plateau and from its gritty back looked down to the oaks and rowan in Stainery Clough and the glint of the Derwent far away near Slippery Stones. Nothing stirred in all that far-off land, virtual silence and white clouds drifting over Bleaklow at this very end of summer.

*Late summer on the
Bleaklow watershed*

*The ruins of Bretton
Clough farm, former home
of William Hawley.*

Bretton Clough, October 1988

This is a magic time to explore the hidden, leafy, golden side-valley above the Derbyshire Derwent. Its busy stream has cut deep into the gritstone outliers west of the main valley, an island of the rough, brown stuff that produces infinitely more attractive landscapes than the pallid, anaemic limestone that surfaces not far off to west and south.

We went up again the other day as the light slanted from the hill-top above Hazelford and were soon lost in the silent country of yellow bracken and burnished oak leaves which the old-time, long gone farmers of this dale would still recognise. Breaking through the last gaudy undergrowth we stepped onto the steep sward, dotted with long-spent thistle skeletons and could again see the familiar stone heaps of Bretton Clough Farm. William Hawley lived here about 1860 and, inspired by the sight of Stephenson's steam locomotive at Chesterfield, set up an experiment in his kitchen to test the power of steam but only succeeded in doing structural damage to his "house-place". The last occupant was Joseph Townsend, an expert rabbit trapper and early this century his snares were said to be "like a parrot cage wi' wires on th' moor above th' house". He left the farm during the Great War and since that day the place has slowly settled into its abandoned slope, known only to hill sheep and ramblers.

Here in this secluded spot the farmers of Eyam drove their cattle during the alarm of 1745, when everyone expected ravages from Prince Charlie's Highlanders. The emergency passed and the cattle resumed their upland pasture. Then we climbed out of the leafy clough and came to solitary Cockey Farm, birth place in 1750 of William Newton whose copious rhymes brought him the title "Minstrel of the Peak". His verse is almost forgotten, as is the origin of the name of his old farm – two cross-eyed men met here and one said "Ah wish thou'd look wheear thour't gooin'", and the other replied "Ah wish thou'd go wheear thour't lookin'".

Hope Woodlands, December 1988

Opposite: winter sundown at the top of Kinder Downfall (E. Hector Kyme)

It had been a perfect day; blue-grey clouds lined every horizon-view but the low sun shone brightly on us. We seemed to sail up the dry, brown moor-side above the Fair Brook onto the Naze, one of Peakland's boldest brows, and so along the ragged crest of The Edge. Long, black shadows were cast far down Black Ashop Moor but up here we were in the brilliance.

Beyond Mill Hill's squelchy summit we went down the dead-heathery way into Hollingworth Clough and across onto the wooded slope of Lantern Pike. An hour later saw us going up again into the sunlight and watching silvery airliners skimming low overhead, en route for the Cheshire plain where mists were already curling. There was still a long way to go and the mid winter sun was heading for the summit crest of Chinley Churn. Our own shadows grew ever longer on the uphill traverse across pastures towards Stony Ford and Edale Cross. Turning up by Swine's Back towards the 2,000 feet contour the sunset glowed and spurred us on towards Noe Stool and over the bleached moor-grasses. The aim was to cross the tiresome peat groughs on this side of the watershed before all light had drained

from the sky; it was a near thing but at last we came to the little stones on the rise called Hartshorn and now the plateau dropped gently away towards the crest of Blackden Edge.

We put up several mountain hares, which scampered off into the gloom as flashes of grey, and grouse growled testily, upset at their night roosts. Now the black void of upper Blackden Clough lay before us, felt more than seen. The stars were out, there was no moon. It was virtually dark now and wisest to traverse some way before going straight down, avoiding vertical outcrops above the sound of tumbling waters.

Negotiating difficult terrain like this in darkness is a time consuming business and always uses lots of energy because one's balance is not so efficient, one's footing never so sure. How often you step on a rock which is actually a foot-deep hollow, or prepare to step down a drop which is level ground! We crossed several plunging torrents, scrambled across rotten faces in the starlight and came at last to the security of Blackden footbridge – all without removing the torch from the rucksack.

North Derbyshire, January 1989

The mild weather continued, not aiding winter wanderings through these short days. The dark clouds tore across the sky, shredded by a warm, west wind; rooks were tossed in the spaces between skeletal trees as we ploughed on towards the great house upon its hill-top. We had covered fifteen miles or so, peered into misty vales and across escarpment country in the hope of glimpsing castles silhouetted against blue-grey cloud banks, without success. Now, as the daylight faded over our high pathway, we saw the parapets and towers ahead. It was no illusion at day's ending, the great house stood in a gap between black plantations and the rooks still swirled.

It was known that the mansion had been vacated these twenty years, decaying and forgotten near the tall trees. We crossed the rutted mud-track to the big farm and entered the narrow, paved path to the church, wading through drifts of dried leaves as we went. The last glimmer of a pallid sundown was reflected on the gilded weather-vane overhead. Then a faint melody came to us, far organ music interrupted by the gusting wind. The church wasn't quite empty and the rosy gleam on the windows was not reflected sunset, it came from within.

Turning down the path we came in sight of the old house again, still silhouetted against that awful sky at day's ending. A last rook crossed in the space between two great sycamores. It was then that I saw it – a light shining from an upper window in a place empty these two decades – how could it be? The sight troubled me as we went on down the lane into ever darker shadows, then I caught sight of the moon rising through a break in the ragged clouds. It must have been a reflection of moonlight we had seen. Then I remembered that all the windows in the great house had long since been smashed or blown in by gales.

Yew Tree Farm,
Bolstersone, looking
southwest towards
Bradfield Moor.

Langsett, February 1989

The day started normally enough; a winter sunrise of orange glow and broken lines of blue-grey cloud. A cold wind blew across the Langsett moors as we went up by Alderman's Head Farm, perched on its exposed knoll surveying all this part of the Little Don Valley. Charollais heifers were grazing, sheltered by a black thicket of hawthorn. At Hartcliff on the open hill-top above 1,150 feet the clouds thickened and rain threatened. We were now out in the open, looking north into the Don Valley as the moor-wind blew ever stronger by the minute.

Our headland, the famous belvedere of west-facing ridge-end called Hartcliff, seemed like a great ship tethered on its taut anchor chain with the gale screaming at its sharp bow as we looked to the massive bulk of Thurlstone Moors where the lowering cloud billows were rolling. The towers of York Minster can be spied from here in perfect conditions, over forty miles away to the north-east across Yorkshire's flatlands. And it is said that Salop's Hawkstone Park has been sighted from here, over sixty miles distant to the south-west, but I've got my doubts because such a line of sight would pass close to the higher parts of Bleaklow and Kinder Scout.

The wind roared around us, contorting the black and blasted sycamores near the stone tower put up about 1851 – little wonder that its roof was ripped off by the wind more than twenty years ago. The only way we made progress on the western scarp slope was by meandering from one stunted tree stalk to the next, until the shelter of a wall was gained. Peering over it into the tearing air stream we could see the new white windmill at Bullhouse, source of great local controversy, and marvel at the blur of triple sails going so fast they were almost invisible. Then the rain came on, level, searching stuff. In our high view over Penistone the sheep took to the wall-sides; we were the only things abroad under the wet, dark canopy.

Abbeydale, March 1989

Opposite: winter snow at the edge of the wood.
(E. Hector Kyme)

The wet snow draped the deep wood for the first time this winter. Dark palls of cloud closed in to shut out the rest of the world as only dismal,snowy weather can. This great swathe of forest remnant climbing the western slopes of Abbeydale was medieval wildwood when Beauchief Abbey was a power-house of the Premonstratensian Order before Henry VIII knocked it about and sent the Abbot, John Sheffield, and twelve cannons packing. During the seventeenth and eighteenth centuries smoke curled above the canopy as charcoal burners produced fuel here for Sheffield's expanding metal trades.

In the heart of the wood I came on that snowy day upon the memorial to George Yardley, "wood collier who was burnt to death in his Cabbin on this place, October 11th, 1786". The poor charcoal burner had friends; a salesman, a gamekeeper, a besom-maker and an innkeeper clubbed together to provide the stone memorial and its pen of iron railings. It's a fitting memorial to this woodland worker of two centuries ago who, in his own small way, helped put the city on the industrial map forever.

At the very top of Ecclesall Wood the trees give way to the open sward of Ryecroft Glen, dappled with sticky snow on this day. I was the only human abroad, it seemed, and sometime later it was the same in the empty, silent trees of the Limb Valley where thick mist wrapped the beech trees. It's fascinating to recall that the ochre-tinged Limb Brook formed part of the important boundary between Mercia and Northumbria in Saxon times, later the Yorkshire-Derbyshire border.

Above the trees stand the ruins of the eighteenth century Copperas Farm, near the place where copperas (green vitriol) was mined two centuries ago. Coal was also worked in this rushy hollow – the blue-grey shale banks can still be seen – where the path went up into the sullen mist. Thoughts of a log fire made a return home in the early dusk all the more inviting.

Looking down Fagney Clough to an arm of Howden Reservoir, with the high moorlands of Derwent Edge beyond.

Derwent Dale, April, 1989

Two classic guidebooks of the thirties by that mountain stalwart Patrick Monkhouse have just been republished under one hardback cover. They are "On Foot in North Wales" and "On Foot in the Peak", the latter particularly appropriate at this time when talk of water privatisation rings loud in these gritstone valleys of great reservoirs. Monkhouse gives advice about avoiding keepers on the sacred grouse moors but steers clear of the ethics of trespassing and the Access to Mountains Bill which was then still a dream.

Later we got Open Country and for most days of the year can roam the brown heights at will. Walk up onto Derwent Edge and the Howden Moors now, though, and you may get a shock. Wire fences are being erected across the slopes in preparation for the privatisation of water supplies. Whatever you may think about profiteering from the supply of nature's most basic essential there is this gloomy prospect of our wild, water gathering grounds reverting to forbidden territory. Who knows what swathes of hillside will soon be hidden

The impounding wall of Derwent Reservoir and the infant River Derwent.

under more boring evergreen plantations? The new water bosses will be in the business for maximum profit, the hill wanderer will not be a welcome adjunct in the wild places – will he be driven to once more consider a pair of wire cutters essential equipment?

As we went along below the crest of Derwent Edge on a recent sunny morning piles of new stakes and rolls of shiny wire were conspicuous on the heather slopes. Will we soon be back in the days of lurking keepers, of ramblers playing hide-and-seek on the great moors where it is surely the God-given right of all to roam? We cannot help being pessimistic at the sight of all those new fencing materials above Derwent Dale. At least, though, the ancient bridleway of Cut Gate, where Hope Woodlands farmers went to Penistone market through the centuries, cannot be closed.

Hawthorn blooms

North Derbyshire, July 1989

Contrary to what many urbanites would have us believe there are still lots of unsullied agricultural backwaters, far from the roar of wide-wheeled cultivators and six-furrow reversible ploughs. The high-angled sunlight of midsummer brings scintillating brilliance to deciduous leaves and the woodland floor beneath them, even at evening the slantwise rays shine strongly through the trunks. It was on such a recent evening that I came down the rushy hollow from Leash Fen, a hollow which winds and deepens as it goes, overhung by stunted hawthorns at first and further down by fine beech and oak. No path comes this way, no muddy track or trampled grasses suggest previous discovery; it's an English paradise.

The sultry air carried echoes of the little brook and songs of happy dunnocks and a cheeky wren. A gate in the wood-edge now gave access to a pasture with a fine stone trough fed by a spout. The farmer was coming down with buckets from his antique, yew-sheltered house to the trough and explained that he had no dealings with water rates and the like.

He thought it might thunder later so kept the cows and calves indoors – "young calves don't like heavy rain on their backs". The water he was carrying was for them. We looked from his stony yard across a tree-filled valley to sunlit fields beyond; it was hard to believe that seventy years ago a quarry was working down there but you can still find rusty saw blades by the stream and my acquaintance showed a slender gatepost fashioned there.

The seventeenth century farmhouse leaned in on itself, supported by a pretty range of buildings. Outside the cowshed a three-legged milking stool stood at the ready, determined fowls were scratching for morsels before the light faded. As I climbed the bridleway it was easy to imagine how quickly a new owner could render this corner of paradise quite sterile, with straightened walls, enlarged windows and a concrete yard devoid of calves, fowls and milking stool.

Cow Parsley (Anthriscus sylvestris) in a north Derbyshire hedgerow, high summer

Longdendale, July 1989

A recurring memory is of a picture in a Victorian book inherited in childhood. It showed a little boy in a sailor suit and a girl with cotton bonnet looking at a lizard basking on a rock where acres of blooming heather were ranged to the blue sky; the title, I remember, was "High Summer on the Moor". It is the epitome of carefree days – childhood's happy highway where we can never come again.

That old picture came to mind the other day as we strayed across the remote northern flank of Bleaklow on a day of clear skies and burning heat. Anyone who wishes to find truly empty ground should traverse this high, tilted tableland beyond the peaty watershed of what is actually Britain's only true desert. We crossed the three ravines of the Black Cloughs in turn and came out on the bold crest of Dowstone Rocks. Here is a magnificent view of Longdendale, backed by the summer green of the mighty uplift of gritstone which culminates in the far summit of Black Hill. As Patrick Monkhouse observed, the Longdendale reservoirs "enhance the look of the valley from a distance, and detract from it close at hand". We kept our distance, and watched the pretty sight of sailing boats on the blue of Torside Reservoir as we climbed the dry, rocky bed of Wildboar Clough. This gives one of the most interesting ways onto the Bleaklow plateau, going up great steps of water-smoothed gritstone between the shady clough walls. Gloomy in winter the cool shade was now most welcome but once above the 1,600 feet contour we came out onto easier ground, and the burning afternoon sunlight.

Here at the empty heart of the plateau we crossed Far Moss, silent under the relentless sun; horizons shimmered on every side. Surely we were the only humans left on the planet. A mountain hare bounded away across the dusty peat heaps and a dunlin piped beyond the bilberry banks. Here was high summer on the moor, but no sign of a lizard.

*High summer on Bleaklow,
looking southeast towards
Derwent Edge*

Wildboarclough, October 1989

Shutlingsloe's arid eastern flank reared above the valley trees once the mist had melted. A pale and cloudless arc of sky overtopped all this hill corner of eastern Cheshire on the morning of the twenty-first annual sheep sale. There was no danger of muddy ruts on the steep sale field this year and the frieze of giant beeches in Crag Hall park were already golden and shedding a burnished shower over the sheep pens.

Later that same day we came over the dusty moor to the head-waters of the River Dane and so by rowans hung with their bounty of bloodied berries to the upper Dove. Not a soul stirred in all that broad country which leads the eye down to the sharp cones of the limestone reef knolls of Chrome and Parkhouse Hills. Everyone, it appeared, was away at the sheep sale. A kestrel sailed over the fields near Hollinsclough village but that was all. There are days at this time of year when all the world seems to stand still; this was one of those days. We looked at golden light on the tiny stone bridge over the Dove upstream of Hollinsclough, embowered with rowans heavy with more fruit. To either side reared banks of dog roses glowing with scarlet hips, promising winter fuel aplenty for blackbirds and thrushes.

Warm sunlight shone on the flanks of Friesians as they swung up the lane for milking in Hollinsclough, silent somnambulists where the dahlias peered from cottage gardens. Soon we had climbed by the source of the Manifold to Flash, England's highest village, and on across the Dane Valley to Cut-thorn Hill in time to see the sun sinking behind Shutlingsloe's cone-top. The velvet curtain of dusk was wrapped around Crag Hall park as we came again to Wildboarclough. The only sound was the bleating of the last sheep being loaded in the sale field, about to start a new life in fresh pastures.

*Shutlingsloe from Crag
Hall, Wildboarclough*

*The derelict Cromford Canal between Ambergate and the
collapsed Butterley Tunnel is rarely trodden by humans now.
Goats, though, browse along the banks at Lower Hartshay.*

Derbyshire, December 1989

The hills take on a washed-out look at this time of year, a result of a damp, clear atmosphere after heavy rain and the paling of dying vegetation on moor and hillside copse. When the December sun slants across high ground the true lie of the land becomes more obvious.

As we went along the high pastures that same low-angled sunlight was catching the great pale upthrust of carboniferous limestone across the deep valley. Quarried on a massive scale in the last century the resulting man-made cliff rears to the Stand on its crest. This began as a viewing tower, put up in 1788 by Francis Hurt of Alderwasley Hall, but proved too attractive to the elements and was shattered by lightning late in the last century. It was the ideal place for the Sherwood Foresters' Regimental war memorial and was rebuilt as such after the Great War. From that day to this a beacon light has flashed across the night sky, visible across a great part of the North Midlands.

As we went along, into the secret woods near Shining Cliff, shuffling through a carpet of sweet chestnut leaves and fruits, the failing light took on a rosy glow through the frieze of tree trunks. The limestone cliff opposite, tower-topped, shone an astonishing pink against rain clouds of darkest blue which had long since drifted away eastwards. A magpie cackled in a tree-top, a tramcar bell clanged far away in the pink quarry (it contains the national tram collection) and those were the only sounds.

In the last light a herd of store cattle came trotting towards us, hoping for food; steam shot from their nostrils in the falling temperature – dragons against the sunset, but disappointed dragons, still just visible ten minutes later as we looked back to their chilly hill-top against the first stars.

Longdendale, January 1990

Just six years ago I wrote here about the high-level waters of Chew Reservoir, hidden away upon the moor-top west of Crowden Great Brook and Laddow Rocks. I referred, I remember, to the pale slants of sunshine picking out the dying edges of moor grasses and was reminded of this recently as the clouds parted to let welcome shafts of light across Bleakmires Moss on the long, almost featureless crest of watershed between Don and Etherow, the backbone of this part of England.

The tentative light might have come from an Ivon Hitchens canvas, or a Frank Auerbach with thick layers of paint approaching sculpture. Then I looked up to see a small, white cloud floating in a pale blue pool of sky and Peter Collis came to mind – up-and-coming, Irish-based artist whose little clouds peep from the edge of steep hillsides, all painted thick and rich and scratched through here and there with lines of detail. Soon the vision had passed, the sun had gone and the slantwise beams with it. We were left on our January moor-side where the grey pall welled up from Longdendale. No red grouse cackled here, no mountain hare put up its ears, no human strode the bogs. We were entirely isolated on that long haul across Upper Dead Edge, looking as we went for the unmistakable broken tooth of the old ventilation tower marking the line of the original Woodhead Tunnel of 1845. Soon we saw its gaunt shape, standing against a grey wash of space above the blackened moor, truly Lowryesque up here so close to Redhole Spring, source of the Etherow which drains Longdendale to flow within a mile of that artist's last home at Mottram.

The failing light brought us down to Saltersbrook Bridge, site of the old Miller's Arms public house where Shepherds' Gatherings were held until the early years of this century. Nothing remains today, only the bridge over the torrent and the pounding traffic on the high road.

The wild road crossing near
Saltersford, upper
Longdendale

Langsett, April 1990

Fears abound locally about the Department of Transport's intention to improve road links across this part of the south Pennines. That old, wild highway crossing northern Peakland between the upper Don and Etherow valleys seems again to be the favourite for improvement (attack is a better word). From the Flouch crossroads above Langsett village this road – often called the Woodhead Pass – heads west as it climbs to the watershed at Fiddler's Green 1,500 feet above sea level. An inn was built here in 1817; a blind Woodhead fiddler entertained clients at the opening ceremony, hence the name of this highest ground. Horses were changed here on the long haul from Longdendale or the Yorkshire side but once the Woodhead railway route opened in 1845 the trade fell away and in 1850 the inn closed down.

Unlike the parallel Snake Road crossing four miles to the south much of the Woodhead route lies across exposed moorland, mounting as it goes onto the highest ground and so far more vulnerable to drifting in blizzards – though less threatened by avalanches than the Snake Road in Lady Clough. At Saltersbrook it twists over the stone bridge at the site of the former Miller's Arms where sheep farmers from both sides of the Pennines met at regular "gatherings". The old time shepherds look out from ninety years old sepia photographs, these and a few tumbled stones are all the reminders we have of a long-gone way of life near the headwaters of Etherow, Don and Porter.

Soon, though, the dunlin and curlew will be returning to the mosses, their call and that of the cuckoo, will drift across the level ground of Longside Moss and Cloudberry Moor under the early summer sky. To think of carving a broader highway across these delectable heights is crazy, the concoction of true Philistines.

Early summer on the hill

North Derbyshire, June 1990

It was the day of the annual pilgrimage to the hill. With the hawthorns drifted over with blossom it was time to drive the suckler herd to the edge of the moor. After a winter in the shed the week outside in the Home Field had already put a sheen on their coats and as we started the journey the sunlight glinted off their flanks.

The first quarter mile is downhill, between high hawthorn banks, to the river bridge in the valley bottom. The calves bounced along, their mothers trotted in keen anticipation, bags swinging as they went. The dusty way curves on through little woods which on that day were fairyland indeed; ramsons and bluebells alternated under the green canopy, the looms of Kirman and Belouch could not come close to the colour patterns compounded of these blooms and the broken sunshine. But now the lane turns up the hill and the relentless climb to the tawny moor begins.

Every year this operation has some excitement in its early stages as a calf or younger cow investigates a weak place in hedge or broken gate. Sometimes we've been delayed half an hour while someone dives into undergrowth to turn an escapee and get it back on the straight and narrow. As the journey progresses, though, energies subside and the pace slows. Now we were on the hot hill, in full sunshine, and tongues began to loll. At the old pond under the shading ash we stopped, cows drank long and deep between the kingcup blooms, calves snatched some milk. Then we were off again between the shiny hawthorns.

The cows' flanks were heaving as we turned along the side-track and out onto the open moor. As we fastened the gate the cows already had their heads down into the bright grasses. Soon the calves had found welcome shade under the wiggins and, as if to welcome the herd to the bright uplands, a cuckoo shouted his greeting from a nearby bough.

North Derbyshire, June 1990

Lines of sight are exciting. They are remarkable, too, for the relatively small number of intermediate sighting points needed to see a great distance across our islands. From the western fringe of the southern Pennines (on Morridge or the Weaver Hills, for instance) it is no problem in clear weather to make out the Wrekin's old whaleback and beyond to the dark spine of the Long Mynd. Standing in the tawny heather on Long Mynd's 1,700 feet summit you can, in favourable atmospheric conditions, make out Cader Idris 50 miles away across mid-Wales close beside Cardigan Bay. Looking several degrees towards the north the sharp profile of Y Wyddfa (Snowdon's highest top) is visible, 70 miles distant. From Snowdon in the right conditions I have often seen the Wicklow Mountains almost one hundred miles across the Irish Sea.

The Queen's Silver Jubilee celebrations thirteen years ago included line of sight beacon fires terminating on Hirta of St. Kilda. On several high points following that summer we came across the charred timbers from those beacon fires. On a hot, still day I ran along the lofty crest of Ben Cruachan and saw the ash remains on the Taynuilt Peak, foreground for that superb panorama over Glen Etive towards the untrodden hills of Morvern and away to the western sea.

But, nearer home, it's always a happy thought to realise that in just three jumps in the right conditions I can see my beloved mountains of Eryri – homeland fields – Axe Edge – Clwydian Hills – Y Wyddfa. What may come as a surprise, though, is that to glimpse the much closer North Sea needs the same number of jumps – Magnesian limestone escarpment – Lincoln Edge – Lincoln Wolds – and then it's often difficult to make out the coast from the lowlier convex crests of those far chalk downlands through the common east-side haze of summer days.

The Derwent Valley from the eastern edges – summer haze

Cruck timbers, Bowsen Barn, Bradfield Dale

Agden Clough, July 1990

Friday afternoon is, I think, a poignant part of the week, especially so when piled, white woolpack clouds drift across a summer sky. All the world seems still then, an old-time peace pervades the air. Some of this is, of course, psychological, a compound of long-gone experience; some of it is tied up with personal perception of the week's structure. Friday comes at the end of the working week, one's expectations reach a high point – exciting things ahead. Somehow the reality never quite comes up to scratch.

So it was the other Friday afternoon, second part of a lovely day of soft air and gliding fracto-cumulus. Swallows slipped and wheeled under silent towers of sycamores on the sunlit hillside, a late cuckoo croaked some way off. We went up the steep ground by ancient Bowsen Barn, sole survivor of a once pretty group of buildings – even the little farmhouse is but a pile of stone and shattered oaken beams. Half the roof was off the barn, revealing the precious medieval cruck timbering; havoc wrought on that gale-swept afternoon six months ago when these east Pennine dales funnelled the blast in some unusual places.

Soon we were at the still and sunny foot of Agden Rocher, where the Huddersfield White rock rears in a long front overlooking dale and moor. We lay between the tumbled boulders and watched the swallows hawking still for flies. The Rocher used to be popular with Sheffield climbers but for some reason it's been left to its own devices for years. The old fun and games don't seem to happen here these days. Anyway, we eventually drifted down by ruined Rocher Head Farm, its house a shambles of toppled stone. It's to be hoped that Bowsen Barn roof is soon put back or it'll join the growing ranks of stony wrecks on these delectable hillslopes.

Ronksley Moor, August 1990

Opposite: the Anvil Stone, Bleaklow Hill, looking northeast.

Going up the narrow confines of Linch Clough, high above the site of ancient Ronksley Farm, we came into the full heat of the summer sun. The air was still, not a cloud in the haze-filled sky. Down below the plantation slopes the stony bed of Howden Reservoir lay burning in the sunshine; only a fraction of its normal water content remained. Soon we were on the moor-top and looking through the murky, shimmering air to the far profile of the Grinah Stones.

No birds sang, no breeze ruffled the first purple heather blooms. It was really too hot to wander here atop the mirage moor. I was reminded that the highest ever recorded temperature in these islands was 98 degrees Fahrenheit on August 9th, 1911, in a summer remarkable for its long heat wave. In that same season a violent electric storm wrecked the top of the fourteenth century spire in my own village; that ancient pinnacle now serves as a bird bath in our garden.

Clouds of brown peat dust rose behind us as we went across the moor. Drought and frost make for easy walking on these gritstone plateaux. We were soon across the tiny clough drained by the Grinah Grain, now barely a perceptible trickle in its rushy bed. The heat intensified as we laboured up to the 1,900 feet contour where the toppled boulders of the Grinah Stones form Bleaklow's boldest brow. In 1627 it was "Graine well Stones", a clear indication that Grinah is derived from the Old Norse word "grein" (a confluence of streams). This rocky headland does indeed overlook at some distance the confluence of several small streams.

Just behind us, to the north, is the secluded hollow of Swains Greave where the Derwent is born close to 2,000 feet. We went down there looking for a mossy recess where we might shelter from the fierce sunlight but found no respite, only further silence and shimmering mirage effects across the moor-top. We learned later that the old record was broken that very day – a temperature of 99 degrees Fahrenheit at Cheltenham.

East Cheshire Hills, October 1990

The early mist had cleared as we came over the hill-shoulder, brushing through the rusty bracken on our way to a quiet side valley where the little farm stood upon its grassy ledge. Even from this distance the signs were easily visible – machinery spread around a field edge, a temporary ring of hurdles near the sheep pens, cars parked near the lane.

Farm sales are often sad affairs; the end of an era, a change of fortunes, termination of a life of toil. Sometimes they are massive affairs, sometimes (as here) quite modest. They are always, though, social events where the cognoscenti discuss world events and market prices and their failing fortunes (always the latter). We came across the last fields and through a stile to the machinery field just as the lantern-jawed assistant rang the bell to draw the company together. Heaps of scrap are always sold first – it would be unwise to be left with rusting metal and rotten timbers as the crowd melted away at the end of the show. We worked slowly round the field as each lot was knocked down or, with no bidder, amalgamated with the next lot.

There are usually a few fascinating bygones and here was a milking stool, incubator, dairy tiles, a pair of stone troughs, paraffin lamps. A life time's possessions dissipated in half a morning, generations of selective breeding broken up in minutes to be carried off to a dozen parishes far from home.

The auctioneer's patter had fallen silent as we re-crossed the hill-slope. The low-angled sun was already hidden behind a rising cloud bank; we made for home in time to see the full moon come up from the east like a great, yellow cheese. The Hunter's Moon – the October moon- was well up in the evening sky as the last light failed and we strode on through the bracken. There was a hint of frost in the air.

The old farm, Dane Valley

Upper Ashop farm, Hope Woodlands, looking up Alport Dale

Hope Woodlands, November 1990

I looked out in the early hours and saw the heavens as sharp and bright as ever I've seen them. The stars were as dazzling as any seen on exciting, early starts from high huts in the Alps, *en route* for lofty summits lit only by a pale moon and those shining stars. This recent early rising under Orion and the Heavenly Twins, though, heralded a long day on high ground near home. We came over Kinder Scout from the southern side and saw a pale dawn from Blackden Edge where grouse calls echoed among the rocks.

As the light grew stronger we made out the dark drape of the Snake Plantation in Lady Clough. Those sombre conifers

On the pond, Alport Castles farm

reminded me of how I'd only recently discovered the age of the uniform plantation in the lower Ashop, on the steep slope between Wooller Knoll and the grassy site of Underbank Farm. The wartime project for the employment of topographical water-colourists called Recording Britain was a "wartime effort at combining culture with restrained patriotism". A total of 1,549 pictures were purchased at that time and have been resurrected at the V & A show which ends tomorrow (November 18th). Though he turned to the abstract later Kenneth Rowntree's contributions are outstanding – and it is his "Underbank Farm, Ashop Dale"

of 1940 which shows the long-gone hill farm looking over the dale-bottom, waiting for the rising waters of Ladybower Reservoir to engulf its lower land. The steep, walled pastures behind the house are newly-ploughed, ready to receive the crop of young conifers which have in the intervening half century become the dismal forest under Wooller Knoll.

It wasn't long, though, before we'd left the valley-slopes and their conifer drapes; out across the blanket bog and cotton moss moors, aiming for the sunlit summit ridge of Bleaklow and clear, far views to the eastern and western lowlands.

The southern end of Wharncliffe Crags, Wharncliffe Lodge beyond

Wharncliffe, January 1991

It's exactly a century ago that those two well remembered gritstone pioneers, Puttrell and Watson, put up the first rock climbs on Kinder Scout. The Promontory on Upper Tor and Primitive on neighbouring Nether Tor may seem tame these days but were a real pioneering effort in "forbidden" territory on the Peak District's best known upland overlooking Grindsbrook. Kinder Scout is not, though, where outcrop climbing began; that honour seems to belong to the long overlooked but once mightily popular Wharncliffe Crags high above the Don valley.

Puttrell, Watson and Co. came here in the early 1880's and put up several interesting routes on what is actually Coal Measure sandstone, not gritstone. It has a good supply of positive, incut holds so techniques required are more akin to those of our volcanically derived mountains than the friction methods of most gritstone crags of the area. Wharncliffe became notorious as Britain's dirtiest climbing ground on account of the copious deposits of soot; the edge lies immediately down-wind of the former Samuel Fox's steel works at Stocksbridge and high above the Sheffield-Manchester "Woodhead" railway. Though the elements have cleaned the rocks in the years since the steel works and railway went electric few climbers come here now.

Looking north along the crest of Wharncliffe the other day the soft, winter sunlight slanted through the silver birches; no living soul came into view. It was a quiet, silent sort of day. What a contrast to early post-war days, when cragsmen came by bus to Deepcar, or by train to Wortley station, and climbed through those birch woods to the foot of the rocks. Others came "via devious leafy glades" from Grenoside and Chapeltown in the east.

As I went along the sunlit crest jackdaws shouted to one another in the trees below, a Swaledale ewe watched me from a rock pillar. The stage was set for Puttrell's ghost to come swinging up from Deepcar, a hemp cart rope slung across his shoulders.

Hope Woodlands, February 1991

One of the saddest facets of the south Pennine scene in post war years has been the demise of the shooting cabin. Before the hordes began to roam the Open Country there were a lot of these cabins left; they are relics of the pre-Great War sporting age. No two cabins were identical, all sited in unique positions with an eye to shelter and convenience for shooting parties.

Railway-borne vandals wrecked some of the most accessible ones, others were abandoned and the elements broke them up at a slower rate. There were some secret cabins, though, hidden away, unknown to most walkers and maintained by gamekeepers. Looking through a thirty year old diary I am reminded of intentions to form a Shooting Cabin Preservation Group. We were loitering in the lonely cabin in Oyster Clough on Bleaklow's southern flank, watching February sunbeams lighting the drear moorscape when we hit on the idea of repairing it.

A month later four of us climbed the little side valley again to put our plans into action. Firewood was carried from the coniferous plantation above the Snake Road, others cleaned out the building and set to work on the wooden gable-ends with sandpaper and green paint. Despite the crackling fire in the iron stove we spent a cold night in sleeping bags and were up early. After breakfast we turned to paint the wooden gutters. Joe Townsend, keeper at Snake Cottage, was upon us without warning. Introductions were stormy but the mention of a colleague's name calmed troubled waters for Joe had helped him photograph birds of prey on the nearby moor. He left us with a curious smile and instructions to bury our rubbish at a good depth. We guessed he'd never before come across queer folk who spent their spare time renovating shooting cabins. The Preservation Group never materialized but Oyster Clough cabin remains in reasonable condition, with traces of green paint on its gable-ends.

Ancient Bowsen Barn's
vandalised roof.

Bradfield Dale, April 1991

Last summer I mentioned the lovely Bowsen Barn high on its tilted ledge above Bradfield Dale and presumed the damaged roof had been caused by January's gale last year. That was not so.

Another manifestation of the lawless age in which we live is the theft of old, stone roofing slates from outlying barns and other farm buildings. Bowsen's ancient cruck barn is the only structure left intact since Sheffield City's philistinism flattened the old house and outbuildings years ago. In their wisdom many grand farms in this and neighbouring dales were brought to the ground, Frost House and Agden among them. These days such vandalism would be unthinkable, certainly there are more people about to register strong objections to the appropriate authorities when they see attacks on the rural heritage.

Meanwhile Bowsen Barn, and Dwarriden above the Broomhead shore in neighbouring Ewden Dale, lie partly roofless, their medieval timbers wet by driven snow and rain. The late Bessie Bunker searched out and described no fewer than eighty seven such cruck structures in the border country of northern Derbyshire and southern-most Yorkshire – she missed one or two, like the barn at Hallfield and Holes Clough in Bradfield Dale. Her efforts in the sixties alerted local authorities to the importance of these peculiar buildings, though several were speedily demolished to avoid awkward planning decisions. All this culminated in her monograph on the subject in 1970; though most authorities disagree with her thesis that cruck buildings in this district originated at the hands of the colonizing Angles in the seventh and eighth centuries. Whatever their date they are ancient (maybe medieval) and the survivors must be maintained with the loving care and attention their venerability demands. Lambs were calling on the steep pastures below Bowsen and lapwngs darting in the April airs above as we traversed from Rocher Head the other day. It was grand to be alive, gazing as we went on towards Bradfield at the shining cumulus castles on high, reflected in the glassy surface of Agden Reservoir; only the vandalised roof of nearby Bowsen Barn put a damper on things.

Lower Small Clough Cabin,
Ronksley Moor.

*The author's mother hoeing
the root crop*

113

*In the hayfield, north
Derbyshire*

North Derbyshire, June 1991

Back in the same spot in the valley where I last worked a quarter of a century ago the hill shapes look the same as ever. The well remembered thrust of green ridge beyond Apperknowle still ends in the conical hump of Glasshouse Hill, wood-topped but with the extra adornment of a television relay mast now.

The broad acres of foreground farmland have metamorphosed to hedgeless playing fields, a few old ash trees stand as brave memorials to ancient hedgerows. In all this green valley there were, twenty five years ago, only two farms – Southcote and Oxclose. My great grandfather was born at the latter in 1830. Southcote remains as a private dwelling, Oxclose was swept away twenty years since. As I look out of the classroom window a sea of bricks and mortar covers the valley sides beyond the oasis of playing field; a huge private housing estate has swept over the land, right up to the familiar horizon where once it was possible to make out the distant silhouettes of grazing cows. A concrete viaduct crosses the mouth of the valley, carrying an endless procession on the Leeds-Exeter trunk road.

I see, too, in my mind's eye, the handful of people who came and went in the green valley. On days of late summer heat Mrs. Elsie Ratcliffe and Mrs. Bennett bent their back in the cornfields, building stooks with the sheaves thrown down by the binder. I still see the old sacks serving as aprons wrapped round their waists, and their bleeding fingers pricked by stubble stalks. At teatime the Friesian herd formed a monochrome caravan along the dusty lane to Manor Farm, passing the old tip where townsfolk often foraged for rhubarb and horse radish. All those years ago the headmaster pointed out that the proposed estate would one day be our very "bread and butter". Such has been the case but it's ironic that my very viewpoint is the place where wallflowers and celery were once grown as part of a course in rural conservation.

Summer heat

*Moving to new pasture,
north Derbyshire*

Only a trickle – taking turns

North Derbyshire, June 1991

A little, white farm stands high on a steep hillside above the Hope Valley. It commands a broad view of that valley and the surrounding rim of lofty hills. Many years ago, before the last war, it was the home of an old established valley family of small-time farmers. The modern town dweller motoring through this delectable country and glimpsing these distant, hillside farms knows little or nothing of their past, of the way of life of the folk who lived up there at the edge of the moors. These long-gone yeomen are now as remote as Red Indians or Bushmen to the urbanite in his sporting hatchback or dressed in purpose-designed finery of some eighties-style ramblers.

The farmer of the white-washed hill farm used to get up at five o'clock every morning to milk his little Shorthorn herd. When he'd hung up the milking stool on the cowshed wall the horse was harnessed and backed into the two-wheeled cart. The churns were thrown up and the equipage descended the fearfully steep track to the valley floor. The churns were unloaded on Hope railway station platform and the farmer set off homewards before the train came steaming in, en route for Sheffield.

On the steepest part of the climb to the farm he would slip from the shafts and walk; he respected all his animals. The wife had washed the milk pail and prepared breakfast by the time the milk had been delivered. Soon, though, the farmer was off down the stony track once more. An eight-hour day in the stone quarry now followed – long journeys to villages beyond the hills or short runs to a nearby builder's yard. Whenever the loaded cart came to an uphill pull the farmer walked beside his horse. He soon washed away the cholesterol he'd taken on board at breakfast, all that home-fed bacon and eggs and butter on his bread.

His niece remembers that he had never put a razor to his face and in old age sported a magnificent silver beard. He never learned to read but this was a closely guarded secret for, whenever he had a document to read in the presence of company, his loyal wife would stand behind his chair while he held the paper and she would read it aloud, as if the better to understand it herself.

When the steep lane got too much for them both they moved to a cottage in Bamford and other farmers occupied the little, white farm. The man who lives there now drives a four-wheel drive sports car and commutes by train to London – I know whose life style I envy most.

More Hall Reservoir in lower Ewden Dale, looking towards Bolsterstone village

Bolsterstone, September 1991

Of all the hill-top villages in this part of the country none sits more solidly upon its ridge than Bolsterstone. Up here the Pennine air seems always fresh because we're almost 1,000 feet above the sea.

The other day we took the ridge-top path that runs eastwards from the village. There wasn't a breath of breeze under a cloudless sky. No sound came to us as we went along through wiry grass burnished by a rainless month; late hairbells still shone bravely, reflecting the sky. Cows were grazing the high pasture over the wall to our left as we sat to look back. The squat tower of the dark-stoned church crouched amongst its graveyard trees but we could see nothing of the medieval castle that once dominated the settlement. Below our belvedere, to the south, More Hall and Broomhead Reservoirs, like the hare-bells, reflected a Mediterranean sky. Far up at the head of Ewden Dale, beyond the reservoirs, the purple profile of the Broomhead Moors dominated the horizon and, now and then, we heard the "pop, pop" of a shooting party on what was, in Edwardian times, England's record breaking grouse moor.

Our immediate ridge-top world was quiet, though. Over the wall a resting cow had her eyes closed and ears back, slowly chewing her cud. An ear flicked off a visiting fly. We were all at peace up here.

Going along further, the deep woods of Wharncliffe came into view, across the great space of the Don Valley, and above the woods the brown pastures of Wharncliffe Chase – highest of stately parklands where once North American bison roamed. We had reached the ridge-end, at the crumpled top of Town-end Common where long-gone quarrying has left complex earthworks covered by desiccated moor grasses. It is a major viewpoint, looking out beyond Stocksbridge and Deepcar across the multi-hilltopped South Yorkshire terrain. We saw, too, the little eminence of Walders Low on the grassy ridge-top, halfway back to Bolsterstone. Here lies an ancient chieftain who has left his name in other places locally; though dead these many centuries, he would surely readily recognize the unchanged grassy ridge country.

North Derbyshire, October 1991

Had you been walking beside the River Wye, where it meanders under Great Shacklow Wood, on a certain day in 1966 you would have witnessed one of the most dramatic natural events in the region this century.

It is said that the Magpie Mine, near Sheldon on the limestone plateau, has been worked for more than three centuries; certainly it was being worked by Thomas Woodruff and partners two hundred years ago. Water always troubled the Magpie lead miners and in a final attempt to solve the problem a sough was driven from the River Wye, under Sheldon village and on to the mine. It took nine years (1872-81) to excavate and helped to drain the 728 feet deep main shaft but the Magpie was never fully viable again, despite various efforts to mine lead up to 1958.

In 1962, part of an air and winding shaft collapsed into the sough. This blocked the drainage but no-one seemed to bother about it until heavy rain in the spring of 1966 caused springs to gush from the hillside in Great Shacklow Wood, high above the outfall of the sough. Pressure continued to build up for several days, culminating in a blow-out of the pent-up flood. Water burst from the slope to leave a 30 feet deep crater. Hundreds of tons of scree and subsoil swept down to the river, partially blocking it. The sough was unstopped and Magpie mine drained but it has never been worked commercially again. It's in the care of the Peak District Mines Historical Society because Magpie represents the most complete remains of lead mining activity in this part of England. There are over twenty open shafts and impressive ruined buildings, including the roofless Cornish engine house and chimney. Seen against a stormy sunset sky the Magpie relics seem apposite; memorials to the ups and downs of the earliest of metal industries – protracted disputes over mineral rights between miners, underground fire, exhausted veins, lack of capital and, back to the sough, the ever present headache of water. That scar above the Wye is a fine memorial to that particular problem.

Gritstone waterfall

Derwent Dale, November 1991

It was one of those magnificent autumn days. A chill wind, cloudless sky and burnished uplands produced a magic landscape as we went up through Shireowlers North Plantation to come out high above the mouth of Abbey Brook Clough. Across this finest of south Pennine side valleys the rowan, birch and oaks of New Close Wood bejewelled our foreground views; beyond and far away were the blue distances of Ronksley Moor and Howden Moor – horizon hills. Beyond the site of the vanished shooting cabins, where dumpy hillocks mark a long-ago landslip, we went down to the secret, rocky floor of the clough and swung up the side of waterfalls quite hidden from the world.

At the largest waterfall we gave up because the rocks were sheathed in ice where a great wall of shadow was thrown down by the right bank. An attempt on the sunlit crag above failed, too. In the end we went round and over Robin Hood Moss to the isolated Wet Stones. What a vista we had on that day, far away to the masts on Holme Moss and Emley Moor and the man-made cumulus of Ferrybridge and Eggborough thirty and more miles off.

On again, and so to Margery Hill, highest point of South Yorkshire. Then there was Cut Gate to cross, the ancient cart track followed by farmers and trader folk between Hope and Derwent Woodlands and Penistone market. It's difficult to believe that a century ago Cut Gate was repaired annually as a horse-way by employees of the Duke of Norfolk and Mr. Thomasson of Grainfoot, Derwent. Writing before the last war, G.H.B Ward suggested that public authorities hadn't spent a penny on repairs since 1900. It would be an adventurous driver that contemplated taking horse and cart on this bridleway now! We went on the ridge-top way, putting up a mountain hare as we came to Outer Edge, and did some scrambling at the Crow Stones with a late, limpid sky above Bleaklow as backdrop for our performance.

Agden Clough, December 1991

The pale winter sunlight flickered on the underside of thin, cold clouds forming a graceful skein over the Emlin ridge. We went up through rhododendron thickets in Agden Clough and looked towards the moor-top and the silvery cloud-skein; a grouse cackled far away then fell silent.

Agden (oak) Wood hangs to the fierce slope overlooking the moor stream as it falls eastwards towards the reservoir and Low Bradfield. Up there, conspicuously perched above Agden Bridge, stands secluded Agden Lodge. It is set about with rhododendron and dark conifers. The sight of it reminds me that great uncle Arnold Muir Wilson bought this estate in 1905 for £7,200 and when he died four years later, leaving a characteristically complicated will, it couldn't be sold until 1920. Then the Public Trustees sold it for £6,700 (including the extra properties of West Knab, Swan Cottage and Walker Edge Farms) at a time when farming was heading for rock bottom and the sporting moors were a luxury that tempted few.

Upstream of Agden Bridge the stream cuts deeply into Rook Cabin Flat and Hobson Moss. Hidden up on the northern side is the ancient bridleway called the Duke's Road, the trackway onto the high moor once maintained by the Duke of Norfolk but now sadly eroded in many places. This track is a useful way onto the Derwent Edge watershed, making for fast and easy progress by day or night. Progress is much slower, of course, down in the clough as we go up beside the plunging stream to the featureless tussock ridge-top of Cartledge Flat. A chilly wind was crossing the high moor when we reached it, the western sky took on the glow of setting sun. On these short days it's easy to finish in darkness but in familiar territory you can make your way home quite well; it's fatal, though, to resort to artificial light, that way there's inky oblivion beyond the beam. An hour later we could make out the glimmer of light in Agden – the Lodge is still inhabited.

Hope Woodlands, January 1992

The deepest snow I ever remember encountering in this part of the country was in January, 1960 when traversing the high ground above this valley. Above about 1,900 feet the surface had been blown clear of much of the loose, powdery stuff but there were lots of groughs where it was necessary to wallow up to the waist. On the whole, though, it was straightforward going on the plateau-top with dramatic views towards the north, where Bleaklow's broad summit ridge lay grey and white under dark snow clouds five miles away.

The long slope down to the Ashop River had an even blanket of frozen snow on it and gravity made the plunging descent relatively easy. An ice-bridge gave access to the far river bank and then the hard work really began. The snow was drifted in broad waves at the edge of the coniferous plantation at the mouth of Oyster Clough; in the uniform light under those thick clouds it was difficult to see where one wave ended and the next trough began. At times the soft dust was at waist level, the next moment I was going up on top of a solid crust. The path that wanders high up along the western side of this hidden valley had sharp-crested drifts that reached twenty feet in places but blue sky showed through an overhead window for a few minutes before the shooting cabin came into view at a turn in the clough.

A barrow-load of snow dropped inside as I opened the door. On the window sill there was a curl of crystals, blown there between frame and glass during the previous night. The panes themselves were frosted over with snail shell whorls and ferny fronds. The empty stove looked black and dead but the cabin was some sort of haven from the blowing dust as the wind got up.

Only thirty feet higher, out on the open plateau, most of the snow had again been swept away so that the going was easy on the frozen, rock hard peat. A line of tracks over the white wavecrests made me envious of the small weight to paw-size ratio of mountain hares.

Oyster Clough shooting
cabin

Sylvan ravine in gritstone country

Rivelin, February 1992

In the days when most folk set out from the nearest tram terminus the deep clough of Wyming Brook was better known than now. The path across the bosky Fox Hagg brought them from the woods on Rivelin's rocky edge to the larger Rivelin Dam near the woodman's cottage. Just beyond you still hear the crashing of falling water. It heralds the eastern end of the little known Rivelin Water Tunnel, one of the great engineering feats of the earliest twentieth century. Constructed in 1904 it brings 10.5 million gallons of water each day from the Derwent Valley through a 4.5 mile long tunnel to Rivelin. This is the total share of nearly 4 billion gallons which Sheffield obtains from the Derwent Valley every year.

The Rivelin Water Tunnel is 6.5 feet high, cut through mainly solid millstone grit in a direct route under the Hallam Moors. The difference in altitude between inlet and outlet is so small that the gradient of the Water Tunnel is only 1 in 3600. In its western half the Tunnel passes through abundantly aqueous rock layers so that half a million gallons of the daily total drains naturally from this strata to swell the Derwent supply.

Lucky the early ramblers who had access to the working after it was completed and before it came into service. Some of them must have made the subterranean short cut between Rivelin and the Derwent Valley near Ashopton to speed their journey into the high hills, or back at the end of the day. When we came across Fox Hagg the other day the soft winter sunlight set the bracken ablaze and played on the birch trunks, then we were past the woodman's cottage and along the reservoir-side. The Derwent waters were thundering from the Tunnel as ever, a string of ochre foam trailed out across the face of Rivelin. The din of falling water stayed with us for some way along the Wyming Brook Drive where the giant conifers were piercing the limpid February sky.

North Derbyshire, March 1992

The hills are alive with mysteries from the past and many of them must lie undiscovered by modern man, some are known but remain unexplained. We know surprisingly little of that so-called dark time after the Romans left our uplands. We don't have much idea, for instance, about the origins of the Pecsaetan, seventh century inhabitants of the area. It's possible that they were Angles who had travelled from the eastern lowlands and settled here in the hills; it's quite possible, though, that they were descendants of people who had lived here from Roman times. We do know that they left their name here and it is still in use as the District of the Pecsaetan.

An area particularly rich in enigmas is the green country of lower Bradwell Dale, tree-dotted and just where the Carboniferous shales give out to the massive limestones. The field path linking Bradwell and Brough comes upon a grassy rampart with a ditch beyond on the northern side. Ancient hawthorns grow upon the rampart, adding to the antique atmosphere. Whatever purpose this Grey Ditch served (and when it was put there) has long since been forgotten and not been rediscovered. Is there a clue in the pastures between Brough and Hope? There lie the important remains of Navio, Roman fort on a grassy terrace above the chilly Peakshole Water – though it might take some finding, so well did the early twentieth century archaeologists put back their excavations. A bit further along is what has been described as "a remarkable and little mentioned relic of the Roman world in the modern landscape". It's a charming, grass covered terrace or shelf above the river and is part of the original Roman route between Melandra Castle beside the Etherow and Navio. There are no signposts here, no information boards or other late twentieth century impedimenta directed at the urbanite that increasingly blight the honeypot areas and effectively demolish the pastorale. Here we can discover our particular paradise, and walking between the cattle may see a local collecting firewood from the storm-bent thorns.

The complex of landslips near the head of Bretton Clough

A selection of books from Sigma Leisure

Explore the countryside with Sigma! Find out more about the north-west of England with our super guide books. We have a wide selection of guides to individual towns from Buxton to Lancaster, plus outdoor activities centred on walking and cycling in the great outdoors. Here are some recent highlights:

Great Days Out! – Derbyshire and the Peak District – Janet Smith; £4.95. *Great Days Out* helps mums and dads enjoy their excursions to both big and small attractions in the area. Companion publications are available for *Great Days Out* in both Manchester and West Yorkshire: £2.95 each.

Sample the delights of country pubs all over England, and enjoy some of the finest walks with our expanding range of 'real ale' books:

☆ PUB WALKS IN THE PEAK DISTRICT
– Les Lumsdon and Martin Smith

☆ MORE PUB WALKS IN THE PEAK DISTRICT
– Les Lumsdon and Martin Smith

☆ PUB WALKS IN LANCASHIRE
– Neil Coates

☆ PUB WALKS IN THE PENNINES
– Les Lumsdon and Colin Speakman

☆ PUB WALKS IN THE LAKE DISTRICT – Neil Coates

☆ PUB WALKS IN THE YORKSHIRE DALES – Clive Price

☆ PUB WALKS IN THE COTSWOLDS – Laurence Main

☆ PUB WALKS IN OXFORDSHIRE – Laurence Main

☆ HEREFORDSHIRE WALKS – REAL ALE AND CIDER COUNTRY – Les Lumsdon

☆ PUB WALKS IN CHESHIRE – Jen Darling

- all 'Pub Walks' books are just £6.95 each. Many more scheduled in this series – ask for our current list.

There are even more books for outdoor people in our catalogue, including:

☆ EAST CHESHIRE WALKS – Graham Beech

☆ WEST CHESHIRE WALKS – Jen Darling

☆ WEST PENNINE WALKS – Mike Cresswell

☆ NEWARK AND SHERWOOD RAMBLES – Malcolm McKenzie

Even more books from Sigma Leisure . . .

☆ RAMBLES AROUND MANCHESTER
   – Mike Cresswell

☆ WESTERN LAKELAND RAMBLES
   – Gordon Brown

☆ WELSH WALKS: Dolgellau and the Cambrian Coast
   – Laurence Main and Morag Perrott

☆ WELSH WALKS: Aberystwyth and District
   – Laurence Main and Morag Perrott

☆ OFF-BEAT CYCLING IN THE PEAK DISTRICT – Clive Smith

– all of our walking and cycling books are currently £6.95 each.

For·long-distance walks enthusiasts, we have several books including:

☆ THE GREATER MANCHESTER BOUNDARY WALK
   – Graham Phythian

☆ THE THIRLMERE WAY
   – Tim Cappelli

☆ THE MARCHES WAY
   – Les Lumsdon

– all £6.95 each

We also publish:

☆ A guide to the 'Pubs of Old Lancashire'

☆ Spooky stories about Stockport!

☆ Myths and Legends

– plus many more entertaining and educational books being regularly added to our list.

All of our books are available from your local bookshop. In case of difficulty, or to obtain our complete catalogue, please contact:

**Sigma Leisure,
1 South Oak Lane,
Wilmslow, Cheshire SK9 6AR
Phone: 0625 – 531035 Fax: 0625 – 536800**

ACCESS and VISA orders welcome – call our friendly sales staff or use our 24 hour Answerphone service! Most orders are despatched on the day we receive your order – you could be enjoying our books in just a couple of days.

AUTHORS: if you have an interesting idea for a book, contact us for a rapid and expert decision. Note that we are not a Vanity press – all of our books earn royalties for their writers.